W9-ALU-100
GRADE
5
MSA Finish Line
Reading

Continental Press

Credits

Editorial Development: Beth Spencer, Megan Bergonzi

Cover Design: Kay Walker

Interior Design: Crystal Crater

Illustrators: Pages 36, 53, 57, 60, 147, 149, 194, James McConnell; Pages 44, 69, 170, 173, 174, 179, Margaret Sanfilippo; Pages 49, 50, 73, 81, 84, 108, 116, 120, 126, 128 (map), 133, 140, 152, 156, Laurie Conley; Pages 76, 88, 100, 103, 106, 189, Rob Williams; Pages 112, 123, 138, 163, Mike Fink; Pages 124, 131, 192, Estella Hickman; Pages 168, 181, 182, Stan Tusan; Page 177, Harry Norcross

Photo Credits: Front cover and title page: Photodisc Collection/Photodisc Blue/Getty Images; Page 41 Special Collections, National Agricultural Library; Page 46 courtesy of Jules Lusignan; Page 63 courtesy of Scholastic; Pages 65, 66 Photodisc, Inc.; Page 93 courtesy of Josie Mowery; Page 101 Corbis Images; Page 110 courtesy of NASA/JPL; Page 128 Photodisc, Inc.; Page 135 © National Anthropological Archives, Smithsonian Institute, neg. #SPC01279200; Page 142 courtesy of Jimmy Carter Library

ISBN 0-8454-4411-5

Contents

Welcome to Finish Line Reading!

Why do you need this reading book? You already know how to read the words in a book or on a computer screen. But reading is more than recognizing words. Reading is *thinking*.

Whether you are reading fiction or nonfiction, you need to think along with the writer. That's how you understand what a writer is trying to say. That's also how you judge what you read. Is it true? Is it complete? Does it answer all your questions? Is it interesting? As a reader, you need to think and judge.

This book was written to help you get ready for the MSA reading test. You've been getting ready ever since you started school. Now you're close to the Finish Line—the test. The best way to prepare is to practice using the skills that will be on your test.

The lessons in this book are in three parts.

- The first part of the lesson introduces the reading skill you are going to study and explains what it is and how you use it.
- The second part is called Guided Practice. You will get more than just practice here, you will get help. You will read a selection and answer questions. After each question you will find an explanation of the correct answer. So you will answer questions and find out right away if you are right. You will also learn *why* one answer is right and the others are not.
- The third part is called Test Yourself. This time you will read a selection and answer the questions on your own.

When you finish the lessons, you will take a Guided Test at the end of the book. You will answer the questions on your own, but you will also find some hints to help you think.

Most of the questions you will answer are *multiple choice*. You are given four answer choices, and you decide which one is best. There are also questions that ask you for a *brief constructed response*. That means you must write a short answer to a question about the selection you have read. You should always look at the selection again before you write. That way you can be specific in your answer.

Now you are ready to use this book. When you finish, you'll be ready for the MSA.

Unit 1: Vocabulary

This unit will help you answer vocabulary questions on tests. You already have a pretty big vocabulary that you use when you talk, listen, read, and write. On a test you will be asked what a word or phrase means. If you know the word or phrase, it will be easy to answer the question. But if you're not sure of the meaning, you need to find another way to answer the question.

There are three lessons in this unit:

1 **Related Words** focuses on synonyms, antonyms, and words with multiple meanings. Knowing how words are related can help you identify the correct meaning of a test word.

2 **Word Parts** includes prefixes, suffixes, base words, and compound words. You can use your knowledge of these word parts to figure out the meaning of a word on a test.

3 **Words in Context** shows you how to use information in a reading selection to figure out the meaning of an unfamiliar word. You will also learn about idioms and about the difference between the denotation (meaning) of a word and the connotation (what it suggests).

Here is a test question from this unit. See if you can answer it.

To come from far and wide means to ______.

A explore a new area

B visit from another state

C ride in a comfortable car

D travel from distant places

This question asks about an idiom, far and wide. You can figure out the answer by thinking about the word *far.* Look for a word in the answer choices that suggests something that is far away. Choice D uses the word *distant,* which means about the same as *far.* So the correct answer is D. Choice B might seem like a good answer, but it is too specific. Another state might be very close. And there are no good clues in choices A and C.

LESSON 1

Related Words

(Objectives 1.D.2.b; 1.D.3.a, b)

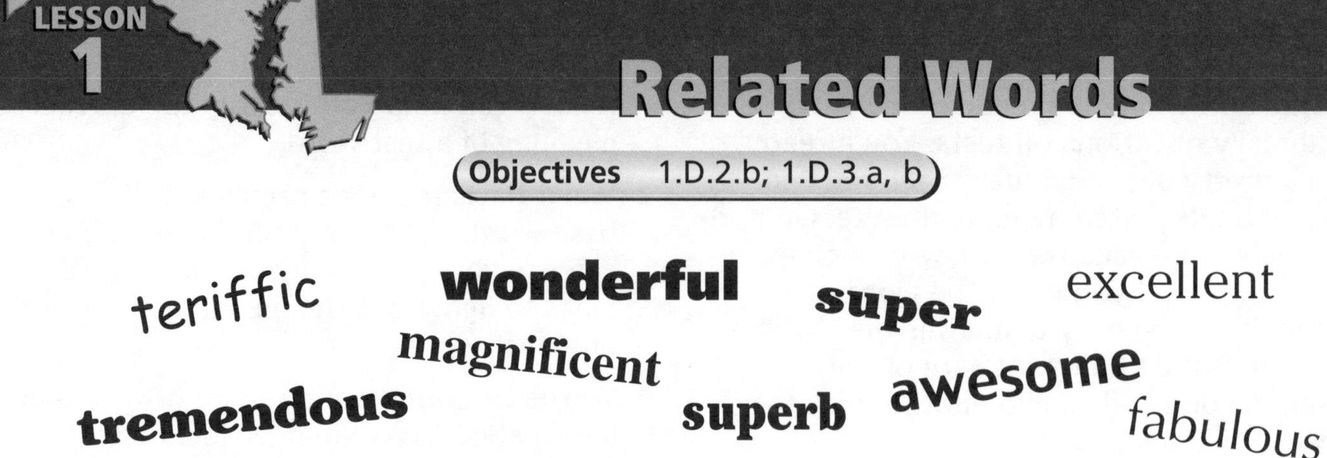

Synonyms and Antonyms

Synonyms are words that mean the same, or almost the same, like the words above. They are all synonyms you can use to describe something very special. Knowing synonyms can help you be a better reader and writer.

Look for a pair of synonyms in these sentences.

Jacquet's cousins reside in Richmond. My cousins live there, too.

If you did not know the word reside, you could figure it out from the synonym live in the second sentence. Both sentences tell about the same thing—cousins in Richmond, and the word *too* is a clue that they are alike. You could exchange the synonyms and both sentences would mean the same thing.

Antonyms are words that mean the opposite of one another. Look for a pair of antonyms in this sentence.

Randal has a severe case of flu, but Rachel only has a mild cold.

The words severe and mild are antonyms. The words *but* and *only* tell you that Rachel's illness is the opposite of Randal's.

See how many antonyms you can name for the words at the top of the page.

______________ ______________ ______________

______________ ______________ ______________

______________ ______________ ______________

______________ ______________ ______________

______________ ______________ ______________

Guided Practice

Choose the word or group of words that means the same as the underlined word.

To be drowsy is to be ______.

- **A** noisy
- **B** ready
- **C** sleepy
- **D** lonely

Which word is a synonym for drowsy? Try to think of a time you have heard or read the word. The word *sleepy* means the same thing. Choice C is the correct answer.

To neglect is to ______.

- **A** ignore
- **B** support
- **C** change
- **D** attempt

Has anyone ever told you not to neglect your homework? The closest synonym is *ignore*. The correct answer is choice A.

An auditorium is a ______.

- **A** noisy gym
- **B** swimming pool
- **C** loud speaker
- **D** large hall

The answer is D. Sometimes one room is both a gym and an auditorium, but not always. An auditorium is always a *large hall,* but it is not always noisy.

Read the following selection and answer the questions that follow.

Rules are important to games. Rules make the difference between just playing and playing a game. If there weren't rules, nobody could win or lose fairly.

The rules for most sports were made up in the distant past. Rules can change, even though such change is infrequent. A rule might be changed to make the game more exciting to watch or to make the game safer for the players.

Choose the word or group of words that means the opposite of the underlined word.

The opposite of <u>fairly</u> is ______.

- **A** unjustly
- **B** foolishly
- **C** unhappily
- **D** correctly

The words *fair* and *just* are synonyms, so <u>fairly</u> and <u>justly</u> must mean the same thing, too. Adding the prefix *un-* to *justly* changes it to mean "not" justly. *Unjustly* is an antonym of <u>fairly</u> because it means the opposite. Choice A is the correct answer.

The opposite of <u>distant</u> is ______.

- **A** apart
- **B** display
- **C** faint
- **D** nearby

You know that <u>distant</u> means far away. Which word means the opposite of far away? Choice D is the correct answer.

Which word means the opposite of <u>infrequent</u>?

- **A** rare
- **B** strange
- **C** often
- **D** abnormal

<u>Infrequent</u> means the opposite of *frequent*, so you should look for a word that means about the same as *frequent*. The closest word is *often*. The correct answer is C.

Words with Multiple Meanings

Some words have multiple, or many, meanings. Although the words with multiple meanings may not be pronounced the same, they are spelled the same. A dictionary lists each meaning separately, usually with a number in front. The word present has more than one meaning. Here are some meanings of the word present:

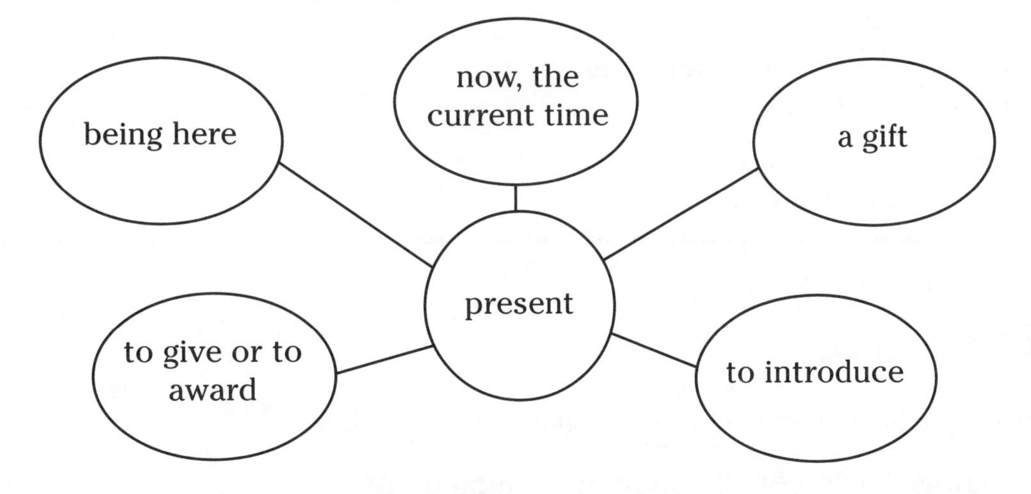

With so many meanings for one word, how can you know which meaning is correct?

Sometimes reading is like being a detective in a mystery. You need clues to find out what a word means. When you read a sentence, you can usually find clues to the meaning of a new word. Notice how a word is used in a sentence. Is it a verb (an action word), or is it a noun (a person, place, or thing)?

The head of the studio presented the television actors with new cars.

You can tell that the word presented is a verb in this sentence. The letters *–ed* at the end tell you that the action happened in the past. Next, try to substitute the meaning for the word in the sentence.

Here are two meanings of present that are verbs. Which one fits the sentence?

1. introduce
2. give

If you replace the word present with each of these meanings, only "give" makes sense.

Write the correct meaning of present for each sentence. Use the meanings in the word web.

SENTENCE	MEANING
The table was piled high with birthday presents.	
Mrs. Garrett, let me present my neighbor, Mr. Tran.	
When the substitute took attendance, all of the students were present.	
At present she is on the city council, but she would like to run for mayor.	

Guided Practice

Read the following selection and answer the questions that follow.

How would you like to be rich and famous and—followed everywhere you go? Many celebrities complain that they can't even buy toothpaste without being hounded by the press. The actors say that they did not sign up for a life of zero privacy. On the other hand, reporters believe they have a right to photograph and write about the details of actors' lives.

In which sentence does the word press mean the same as it means in the paragraph?

- **A** The last step of the directions is to press the green button.
- **B** You will have to press your pants before you can wear them.
- **C** The press are gathering to take notes on the president's speech.
- **D** There were so many people that Tim got lost in the press of the crowd.

The first clue to the meaning of the word press in the paragraph is the word *the,* which tells you that press is being used as a noun. Only choices C and D use the word press as a noun, and only choice C is talking about newspaper or television reporters. Choice C is the correct answer.

In which sentence does the word right mean the same as it means in the paragraph?

A The senator felt that voting for the new law was right.

B All citizens have the right to vote for the candidate they choose.

C It was the right time for the party to propose a new candidate.

D To find the park, go two blocks down the street and turn right.

Look for a sentence that uses the word right in the same way as it is used in the paragraph. In the paragraph, a right is a claim. Reporters feel they are entitled to the freedom of writing about actors. Only choice B is correct.

In which sentence does the word lives mean the same as it does in the paragraph?

A The president's family lives in the White House.

B Many people spend their whole lives in one place.

C The senior play was broadcast live on cable TV.

D Grandma lives for the day she can go home.

The correct answer is B. Lives is a noun in B, as it is in the paragraph. In A and D, lives is a verb, and in C, the word *live* is an adverb.

Test Yourself

Read the following selection and answer the questions that follow.

Storytelling may be entertaining, but for the Navajo people, it is also a way to preserve their history and traditions. The Navajo are an ancient people who live in the deserts of the Southwest. They live simply, guided by the principles and beliefs of their ancestors. These Native Americans pass down their history by telling stories. By listening to stories of the traditional ways, young people learn about the values, culture, and history of their people.

1 The word entertaining means ______.

A fun

B cute

C grand

D cheerful

2 To live simply is to live in a way that is ______.

- **A** busy
- **B** noble
- **C** plain
- **D** noisy

3 To preserve is to ______.

- **A** keep
- **B** praise
- **C** measure
- **D** command

4 The word values means ______.

- **A** facts
- **B** habits
- **C** victories
- **D** principles

5 A tradition is ______.

- **A** an idea
- **B** a custom
- **C** a settlement
- **D** an instruction

Read the following selection and answer the questions that follow.

Of all the many founders of the United States, James Madison lived the longest. The "Father of the Constitution" and our fourth president, Madison survived well into his 80s. In the last years of his long and busy life, Madison was ill. Because of his illness, he rarely left his home. But his mind was as sharp as ever, and he spent much of his time dictating his memoirs.

One afternoon, as he was lying on a couch and dictating to his secretaries, Madison had a coughing fit. The secretaries rushed to his side to help. "Perhaps you could speak more easily if you sat up," said one.

"Oh, no," said Madison. "I have always spoken more easily when I was lying."

1 The word survive means the opposite of ______.

A thrive

B perish

C disgrace

D surrender

2 The word ill means the opposite of ______.

A lonely

B instant

C healthy

D delicate

3 The word rushed means the opposite of ______.

A raced

B strolled

C hurried

D stumbled

4 The word easily means the opposite of ______.

A angrily

B rapidly

C with equality

D with difficulty

Read the following selection and answer the questions that follow.

The celebrated Mexican artist Frida Kahlo was born in 1910. Her colorful, dreamlike paintings had an unusual beginning. When Frida was 16, she was hurt in an accident. While she was in the hospital, Frida began to paint. Painting helped her to recover. Throughout her life, Frida struggled with pain and other health problems. She never stopped painting. Painting became more than just a way to recuperate. It was how she learned to express herself. Her paintings were strange and wonderful portraits. She painted many self-portraits to reveal different parts of her own personality. Her paintings also reflected her Mexican culture and heritage.

1 In which sentence does the word celebrated mean the same thing that it means in the paragraph?

A They celebrated her birthday with a party.

B We all went out and celebrated after the show.

C The movie was made by a celebrated director.

D The story celebrated the idea of lasting friendship.

2 In which sentence does the word express mean the same thing that it means in the paragraph?

A They were late, so they had to take the express bus.

B It is faster to use express shipping, but it costs more.

C He had trouble finding words to express his feelings.

D It is the teacher's express wish that we study the chapter.

3 In which sentence does the word reflected mean the same thing that it means in the paragraph?

A He reflected on the subject before making a decision.

B The performance reflected the cast's talent and hard work.

C Their faces were reflected in the glass window.

D The water gleamed with reflected light.

Objective 1.D.3.b

Prefixes, Suffixes, and Base Words

Many words are made up of different parts. They include **prefixes**, **suffixes**, and **root** or **base words**. If you know what some or all of the parts mean, you can usually figure out the meaning of the word.

Prefixes

A **prefix** is a word part added to the beginning of the word. A prefix changes the meaning of a base word to make a new word. The prefix *un-* means "not." If you add the prefix *un-* to the word happy, you make a new word that means "not happy."

Most prefixes come from Latin or Greek words. For example, the prefix *tri-* is from the Latin word that means three.

WORD	PREFIX + BASE	MEANING
triangle	*tri* + *angle*	a shape with 3 angles
tricycle	*tri* + *cycle*	a vehicle with 3 wheels
tricornered	*tri* + *cornered*	describes something that has 3 corners

Prefix Chart

Prefix	Meaning	Example
bi-	two	bicycle
dis-	not	disappear
extra-	beyond	extraordinary
in-	in or not	independent
mis-	bad or not	mistreat
multi-	many	multiply
non-	not	nonsense
re-	back, again	review
sub-	under	submarine
trans-	through, over, across	transportation
un-	not	unusual
uni-	one	unicycle

Match a prefix with each of these base words to make a word that fits the new meaning.

PREFIX	BASE WORD	NEW MEANING	NEW WORD
	harmed	not harmed	
	continue	not continue; stop	
	certain	not certain	
	merge	go under	
	gain	gain back	
	fiction	not fiction; true	
	spell	spell incorrectly	

Guided Practice

Answer the following questions.

The word unlikely means ______.

- **A** very likely
- **B** not likely
- **C** more than likely
- **D** likely

The prefix *un-* means "not." So unlikely means "not likely." B is the correct answer.

Someone who is bilingual ______.

- **A** knows two languages
- **B** understands one language
- **C** reads three languages
- **D** speaks several language

Since the prefix *bi-* means "two," the only answer that can be correct is choice A.

A subway is a train that goes ______.

- **A** over the ground
- **B** over the water
- **C** over a bridge
- **D** under the ground

The correct answer is D. *Sub-* means "under" so a subway train must go under the ground.

Suffixes

A **suffix** is a word part added to the end of the word. A suffix also changes the meaning of a word.

When it comes to sports, Kaitlyn is fearless.

You know what fear means. The suffix *–less* means "without," so you can figure out that Kaitlyn does not have any fear about playing sports.

Some suffixes change words to different parts of speech. Suffixes can change nouns (people, places, or things) to adjectives, or describing words.

WORD		SUFFIX		NEW WORD
break *verb*	+	*-able*	=	breakable *adjective*
peace *noun*	+	*-ful*	=	peaceful *adjective*
sad *adjective*	+	*-ly*	=	sadly *adverb*
soft *adjective*	+	*-en*	=	soften *verb*

Suffix Chart

Suffix	Meaning	Example
-able	able to, tending to be or do	comfortable
-ance	state, condition, or action	attendance appearance
-en	to cause to be	widen
-ful	full of or able to	thankful
-ish	being like	foolish
-less	without	fearless
-ly	like or in the manner of	properly
-ment	the act of or result	establishment
-ous	full of	humorous
-tion	the act of	celebration
-y	like or tending to	rusty

Match a suffix with each of these words to make a word that fits the new meaning.

WORD	SUFFIX	NEW MEANING	NEW WORD
harm		without harm	
noise		like noise	
admire		able to be admired	
danger		full of danger	
length		to make longer	
agree		act of agreeing	

Guided Practice

Answer the following questions.

The word purposeless means ______.

A like a purpose

B having a purpose

C purposeful

D without a purpose

The clue to the answer is the suffix *-less* which means "without." It tells you that the answer must be D.

The word fatherly means ______.

A being a father

B having a father

C like a father

D without a father

Since the suffix *-ly* means "like" or "in the manner of," fatherly must mean "like a father," choice C.

The word hopeful means ______.

A able to hope

B the act of hoping

C without hope

D like hope

The suffix *-ful* means "able to." Hopeful must mean "able to hope."

Base Words

Prefixes and suffixes must be added to **base words** in order to make new words. If you know what the base words mean and you know what different suffixes and prefixes mean, you can usually figure out the meaning of new words.

The students were so mischievous that the class had become unmanageable for the substitute teacher.

The word unmanageable has the prefix *un-* and the suffix *-able* added to the base word manage. *To manage* means to control or to be in charge of something.

When the prefix and suffix are added, you know that the word is describing something that cannot be managed. This web shows more words that have the base manage:

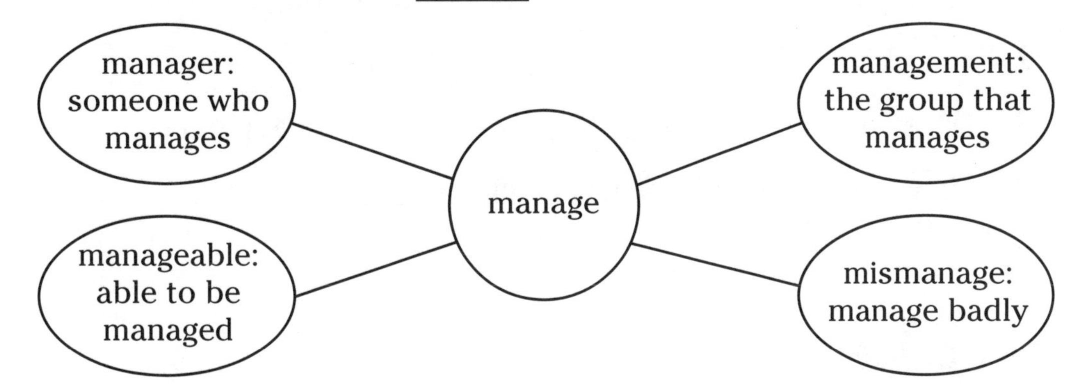

Choose the correct word for each sentence below.

1 Dad asked to speak with the ______________ of the store.

2 Some said the bank was closed down because it had been ______________.

3 The hotel has a new owner and is under new ______________.

4 Two dogs are ______________; three dogs are not.

The word connect is also a base word. If you know that *to connect* means to put together, you can figure out the meanings of many words that have the same base word.

A service representative came for the reconnection of our cable service.

The prefix *re-* tells you something is being done again; the suffix *-tion* means the new word is a noun about something being done.

Here is a web that shows more words with the base connect:

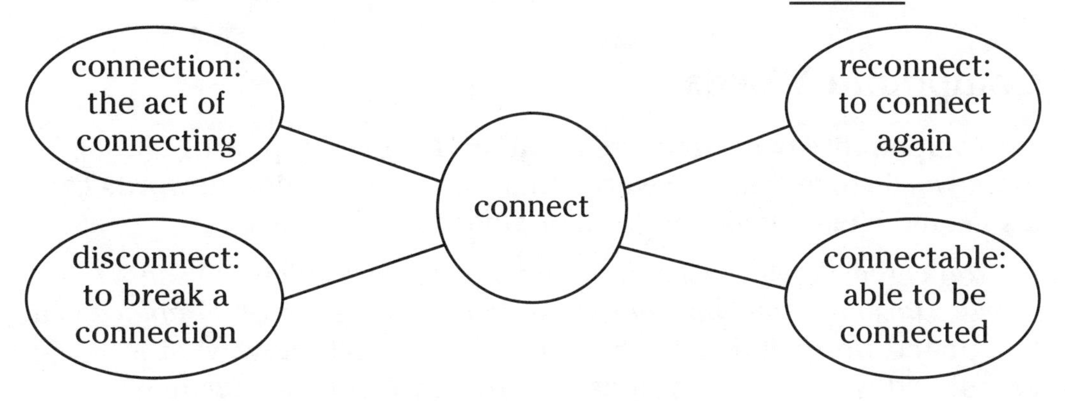

Choose the correct word for each sentence below.

1 You must ______________ the computer during a storm.

2 The DVD player is ______________ to the television.

3 The two trains make a ______________ in Philadelphia.

4 After the storm an electrician came to ______________ our service.

Guided Practice

Answer the following questions.

A person who has a disability _____.

A is always late

B will do more than most people

C cannot do a certain thing

D has a special car

The base word of disability is *able*. If you have an ability, you can do something. The prefix *dis-* means "not." So, someone with a disability cannot do something. C is the correct choice.

An unacceptable package _____.

A will not be taken

B is mislabeled

C cannot be changed

D is not in good condition

Look for the base word *accept*. You know that to accept something means to take it, and the prefix *un-* means "not." All of the answer choices are negative, but only choice A has the meaning of the base word.

Compound Words

Compound words are words that are formed by putting two or more words together. The words that make up compound words can also stand alone, unlike prefixes or suffixes.

You can make several compound words from the word *sun: sunset, sunshine, sunlight, sunrise, sunroom,* and *sunroof. Fireplace* is a compound word, and so is *afternoon*. If you don't know what a compound word means, you can try to figure out the meaning from looking at the words that make up the compound word.

Here are some compound words that you probably know.

WORD		WORD		COMPOUND WORD
night	+	fall	=	nightfall
sales	+	person	=	salesperson
back	+	pack	=	backpack
home	+	work	=	homework
day	+	time	=	daytime
house	+	hold	=	household

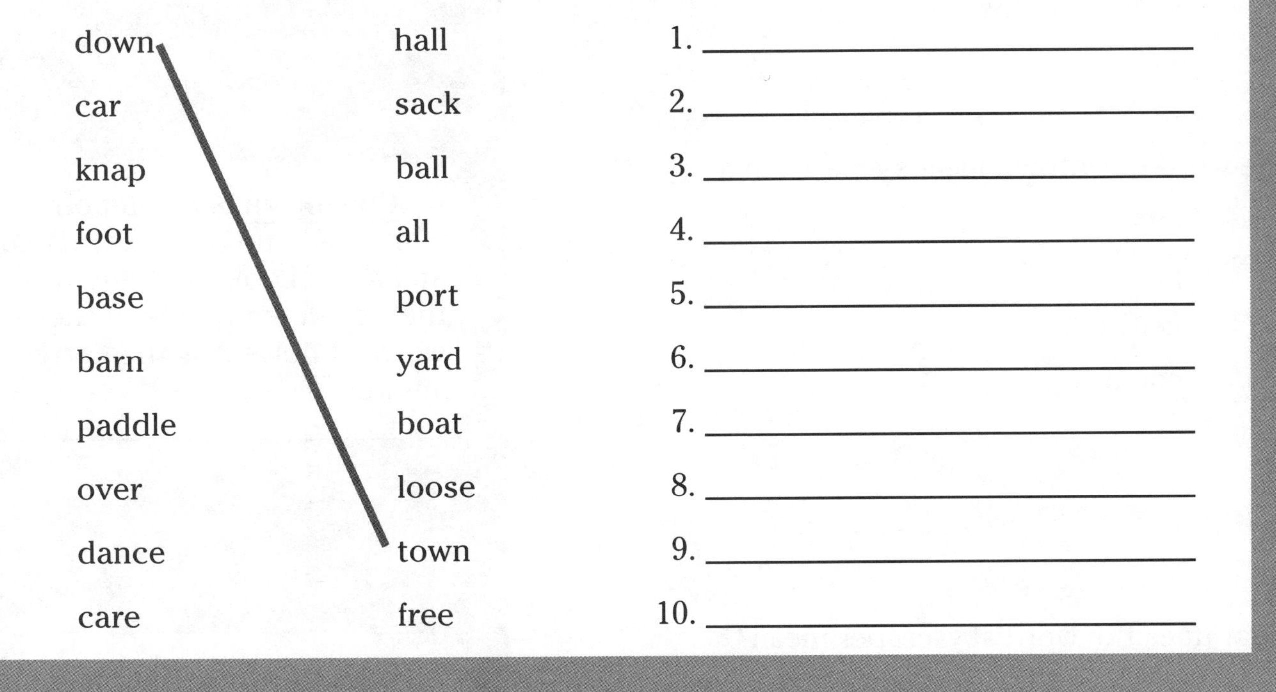

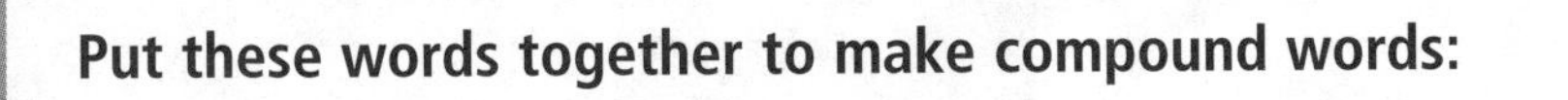

Put these words together to make compound words:

down	hall	1. ______
car	sack	2. ______
knap	ball	3. ______
foot	all	4. ______
base	port	5. ______
barn	yard	6. ______
paddle	boat	7. ______
over	loose	8. ______
dance	town	9. ______
care	free	10. ______

Guided Practice

Read the following selection and answer the questions that follow.

When my family moved to upstate New York, I was only a little girl, but I was old enough to miss the city, especially all of the sights and sounds. I missed the hustle and bustle downtown, with people rushing in and out of stores. I missed the honking taxis and the glow of streetlights. I missed our cozy apartment in the tall skyscraper, so high that I felt as if we lived in the clouds.

The word upstate means the part of the state that is in the ______.

A east

B west

C north

D south

Look for the word that is related to the word *up*. We sometimes talk about the northern direction as if it were located above, or up from, the southern direction. Choice C is the correct answer.

The word downtown means an area in a ______.

A city

B park

C field

D country

Downtown is a compound word made up of the words *down* and *town*. Look for the choice that is related to one of these words. Choice A is the correct answer.

What does the word skyscraper mean?

A a new house

B a wide road

C a public place

D a tall building

Look for words that have to do with something that might "scrape the sky." Only something that is tall could be a skyscraper. Choice D is the correct answer.

Test Yourself

Read the following selection and answer the questions that follow.

Although it was two years ago that I traveled to Asia, my first impressions are still the strongest. Since returning to the United States, I've told the story of my trip to countless relatives and friends. They were all curious about what I saw and asked all sorts of questions. "What was the most beautiful sight?" my grandmother wanted to know. "Did you like the food?" asked my cousin, who wants to be a chef. "Did you learn any of the languages?" wondered my best friend, a writer. "Were the people friendly?" my mother questioned.

At first I answered easily enough, but presently I came to understand that each question had multiple answers. There is so much to tell about this fascinating part of the world. Now when I tell the story, I always begin by describing my first impression. In this way, I try to give a true reflection of what I saw.

This is how my story begins: I rode from the airport in a taxi on a busy highway into the downtown area of a large city. The scene will remain forever in my mind. There were so many people! Thousands of bicycles and brightly colored scooters flowed in the broad streets. I stared in amazement. I would never forget this exciting sight.

1 To <u>disappear</u> means to ______.

A go out of sight

B move back

C show again

D wait for a turn

2 The word <u>countless</u> means ______.

A some

B every

C a certain number

D a very large number

3 The word <u>beautiful</u> means ______.

A like beauty

B full of beauty

C without beauty

D acting with beauty

4 What does the word <u>multiple</u> mean?

A all

B none

C some

D many

5 An <u>airport</u> is a place where ______.

A travelers get together

B packages are shipped

C cars and trains are stored

D planes land and take off

6 What is a <u>highway</u>?

A a clearing

B a building

C a main road

D a parking lot

7 To last <u>forever</u> means to ______.

A fade away

B stay always

C come and go

D disappear suddenly

8 The base word of <u>unchangeable</u> is ______.

A able

B unchanged

C hang

D change

Words in Context

Objective 1.D.3.a

Your vocabulary is made up of all the words you know. You use many words when you speak and write, but you know even more words than the ones you use. Those are the words you understand when you listen or read.

Even if you don't know a word, you can often figure out its meaning from other words in the sentence or paragraph. These words are **context clues**.

Read this sentence from *The Phantom Tollbooth.*

"What did they all do?" the Humbug inquired, suddenly taking an interest in things.

You may know that the word inquired means "asked." If you didn't know the word, you could figure out its meaning from all the other words and ideas in the sentence. In this sentence, you have two context clues: the word *what* and the question mark. These clues tell you that the Humbug is asking a question, so inquired must mean "asked."

Punctuation, such as the question mark in the sentence about the Humbug, may not always give you a clue. Usually, the context clues will be **synonyms**, **examples**, **definitions**, and **descriptions**.

Type of context clue	Synonyms	Examples	Definitions	Descriptions
What they do	have nearly the same meaning	show what a word means	tell what a word means	tell more about a word

Synonyms

A sentence or paragraph might use two synonyms, or words that have meanings that are nearly the same. If you know the meaning of one word, you can figure out the meaning of the other.

> Matt and Ryan raced for the finish line, but Ryan tore ahead and broke the ribbon.

The words raced and tore both tell about people running a race. Even if you didn't know the meaning of tore in this context, you could figure out the meaning. Ryan went ahead of Matt and won the ribbon, so he must have run very fast. In this sentence, tore means the same as raced or "ran very fast."

Examples

Some sentences or paragraphs give examples that help show what a word means. Look at the word communal in the first sentence below. Can you figure out what it means from the sentence that follows?

> Getting ready for a picnic is a communal effort. Mom makes the sandwiches and salads; Dad puts the drinks in an ice chest; I pack the paper plates and napkins; and Rory collects the games.

What does the word communal mean? The examples show that everyone is helping to get ready for the picnic. You can figure out that communal means "everyone working together."

Definitions

Definitions are another kind of context clue. Look for the definition in these sentences:

> The sky over the bay was cerulean, the kind of blue you see only on a clear, sunny day. It filled the sky and seemed to go on forever.

Cerulean is a word that you may not see or hear very often. But you can still figure out what it means because the sentence gives you a definition: "the kind of blue you see only on a clear, sunny day." You can tell that cerulean means "bright blue."

Descriptions

Sometimes a sentence will have a description to tell you what a word means. Do you see the description in this sentence?

> Mr. Cory is proud of his authentic Civil War musket that had been carried by a soldier in the Battle of Antietam.

The word authentic means "real." The sentence gives you a description of the history of the musket. Because the musket had been carried by a soldier, you know that it is not a fake.

Guided Practice

Read the following selection and answer the questions that follow.

To get a pilot's license today, you have to be at least 17 years old. You also have to pass written and flight tests, and have flown a certain number of hours. In 1784, when there were no such rules, thirteen-year-old Edward Warren, a boy from Baltimore, grabbed the chance to ride in the first balloon that rose above American soil.

The balloon was launched by Peter Carnes. Carnes wanted to pilot the balloon himself, but he feared his weight was too much for the balloon. When Carnes asked for volunteers, Edward Warren came forward. Carnes sent him aloft, where birds soared and clouds drifted. It had been a sacrifice, but Carnes surrendered his dream of flying in order to make sure the balloon got off the ground.

To launch means to ______.

A send off

B turn on

C hold down

D take away

> When you read the paragraph, you can find an example that tells you what launch means. Carnes "sent him aloft" is a context clue. The correct answer A.

The word volunteer means ______.

A an experienced pilot

B someone who offers to do a job

C someone who doesn't weigh a lot

D a person under the age of 17

> To answer this question, look at the phrase that means the same thing: "Edward Warren came forward." Choice B is the correct answer.

To surrender means to ______.

A measure

B surround

C long for

D give up

Look back at the sentence that has the word surrender. You see the word *sacrifice,* which is a word that means about the same as surrender in this sentence. Choice D is the correct answer.

Idioms

Idioms are phrases that have a meaning that is not related to the actual meaning of the words in the phrase. Read this sentence.

Because language changes very quickly, new idioms pop up every day.

The actual meaning of the word pop is to burst. That meaning does not fit here. In this sentence, the phrase pop up is an idiom that means "appear."

Here are some other idioms you might know.

Talking until you are blue in the face		to talk for a long time without convincing anyone.
To shake a leg	**MEANS THE SAME AS**	to hurry up.
To see red		to be angry.

See if you can recognize the six idioms in these paragraphs.

"Don't try to pull the wool over my eyes!" Mom said. "You've been hanging out with Kim again, haven't you?"

I knew she'd hit the ceiling when she found out. I had to come clean. "It's true," I said. "But, Mom, Kim's a new person now. She's really turned over a new leaf."

You probably know the meaning of the idiom to hang out with. Try to match the other idioms with these meanings:

to hide information from or deceive

someone who has improved

to change from bad to good

to get very angry

to tell the truth

Guided Practice

Read the following selection and answer the questions that follow.

Mamie Johnson was a star in more ways than one. Born in South Carolina in 1935, she studied engineering at New York University when women who studied engineering were about as scarce as hen's teeth. Mamie went on to work as a nurse. But she is most famous for shining on the baseball field. Nicknamed "Peanut" Johnson, Mamie was a pitcher for the long gone Negro American League.

When she made her mark on the field, Mamie was only 19, and weighed only 105 pounds. But anyone who saw her play would have said she was worth her weight in gold. She got her nickname from a batter on another team. The batter teased Mamie by saying, "How do you expect to strike anybody out? Why, you're no bigger than a peanut!" Mamie got the last laugh when she struck that player out with her curve ball.

The phrase as scarce as hen's teeth means that women who studied engineering then were ______.

- **A** brave
- **B** famous
- **C** athletic
- **D** unusual

The phrase as scarce as hen's teeth is an idiom that describes something uncommon. The correct answer is D.

The phrase worth her weight in gold means that Mamie was ______.

- **A** a good batter
- **B** a valuable player
- **C** young and rich
- **D** heavy and strong

To answer this question, think about what the phrase worth her weight in gold means. A thing made of gold is valuable. Choice B is the correct answer.

What does the phrase to get the last laugh mean?

- **A** to make a joke
- **B** to hit a home run
- **C** to triumph in the end
- **D** to make a dream come true

To answer this question, think about what had happened. After the other player made fun of Mamie, Mamie struck that player out. To get the last laugh is an idiom that means the same as choice C, to triumph in the end.

Connotation and Denotation

The **denotation** of a word is its actual meaning, the thing or quality that the word stands for. The word house is a good example. House simply means a building in which people live. But the **connotation** of a word includes ideas and feelings beyond the actual meaning of the word. For example, the word home means more than just a house. Home makes you think of a cozy place to live. Home might make you think about warmth and comfort and families.

The chorus of the song "Home on the Range" gives some examples of words that have meaning added to the actual meanings.

Home, home on the range
Where the deer and the antelope play
And seldom is heard a discouraging word
And the skies are not cloudy all day.

You know the added meanings of the word home. Think about meanings the word range might have, meanings such as freedom, wilderness, nature, and wide, open spaces. The word cloudy describes the skies, but it also describes a mood or a feeling of being troubled. The last line of the chorus suggests that life is happy and carefree on the range.

Try to match the word or phrase to the meaning it connotes.

WORD OR PHRASE	DENOTATION	CONNOTATION
apple pie	a pastry	____________
true-blue	a color	____________
an owl	a bird	____________
a star	a body of light in space	____________
a mule	a farm animal	____________
a heart	an organ that pumps blood	____________

loyal
kind
neat
stubborn
successful
wise

Guided Practice

Read the following selection and answer the questions that follow.

In the 1700s, the ships of Spanish explorers roamed the earth and ruled the seas. Legend is that noble ponies from one such ship swam ashore to escape a shipwreck, but the truth about the ponies of Assateague and Chincoteague is not so romantic. Shaggy and cuddly, the ponies are actually tiny horses. They are descendants of horses that were moved to the islands hundreds of years ago. The horses were relocated by owners who wanted to avoid paying taxes on their horses or who did not want to keep them behind fences. These "ponies" became wild over time.

The wild horses owe their small size to poor nutrition. They live on the grasses and twigs flavored by the sea, with a little seaweed thrown in. The horses become so thirsty from the salty food that they drink large amounts of water, which gives them their plump shape.

The word roamed means to have traveled ______.

- A freely
- B easily
- C slowly
- D skillfully

The word roam has a connotative meaning that makes you think of moving freely over a large area. The correct answer is choice A.

What does the word cuddly mean?

- A free
- B cute
- C wild
- D furry

The word cuddly describes something you would want to hug or *cuddle*. This word also has a connotative meaning that makes you think of a teddy bear or another stuffed animal. You can tell that the correct answer is B, cute.

The word plump means that the ponies are ______.

- A fat and dirty
- B wide and bony
- C strong and light
- D soft and round

Look back at how the ponies are described in the selection. Then think about synonyms for the word plump. Plump means almost the same as *fat*, but the word plump has added meanings of softness and pleasantness. Choice D is the correct answer.

Test Yourself

Read the following selection and answer the questions that follow.

During winter vacation, Jeff's family comes from far and wide to gather at the square brick house in Frostburg. The house buzzes like a beehive from all the activity. Soon all of the aunts and uncles and cousins settle into the familiar routine of family customs and traditions. Meals are in the dining room, with Grandpa at the head of the table. At night, the children snuggle in nests of blankets on the carpets in front of the fireplace, whispering stories and laughing until lights out.

When snow flurries drift in the air, it is time for sledding and snowball fights. Everyone gets in on the act. Jeff's grandparents scour the attic, peering into every nook and cranny, for sleds, snowshoes, and extra gloves, scarves, and mittens. All of the cousins are herded out into the cold to make forts and snowballs. There is always a competition for the biggest snowman. Last year, Jeff won. His snowman was an impressive height: six feet of hard-packed powder!

1 To come from far and wide means to ______.

A explore a new area

B visit from another state

C ride in a comfortable car

D travel from distant places

2 What does the word routine mean?

A a long vacation

B a busy calendar

C a set of usual activities

D a group of cheerful relatives

3 The phrase buzz like a beehive means that the house ______.

A seems busy and noisy

B is crowded with insects

C has honey in the pantry

D is dangerous for children

4 What does the phrase at the head of the table show about Grandpa?

A that he usually is served last

B that he is taller than the others

C that he sits in the place of honor

D that he is the first person to sit down

5 The word snuggle shows that the children are ______.

A cozy and warm together

B playing games at bedtime

C pushing and shoving each other

D lonely and missing their homes

6 What does the phrase to get in on the act mean?

A to interfere

B to participate

C to have a part in a play

D to compete with others

7 What does the word scour mean as it is used in this paragraph?

A to scrub very hard

B to clean up a mess

C to make very bright

D to search very carefully

8 To <u>herd</u> means to ______.

A to lead

B to send

C to carry

D to permit

9 What does the word <u>impressive</u> mean?

A impatient

B mysterious

C remarkable

D imitation

Unit 2: Comprehension

Comprehension means "understanding." On a test, you have to understand how the words go together and what it all means. This unit will guide you through seven important comprehension skills.

1 **Main Idea** The main idea is the reason an author has written something. When you finish reading something, you should be able to say "The author's main idea is ____________."

2 **Details** All the specific information that a writer includes is there so the main idea will be clear. As you read, the details will give you a sense of the main idea.

3 **Inferences and Conclusions** This is where the author wants *you* to be part of the story or article. You have to put details or references together to make inferences and draw conclusions about what you are reading.

4 **Making Predictions** When you watch a television program, you are probably guessing what will happen next. That's true when you read, too. Predicting what will happen next means you understand the parts and details of what you're reading.

5 **Sequence and Chronological Order** It's not always easy to figure out the sequence or order things happen in a reading selection. Clue words and hints can help you.

6 **Prior Knowledge** Prior means "before." So prior knowledge means what you already know before you begin to read. Sometimes you have to think about it (Where *is* Disney World?), but often it's right at the top of your head.

7 **Summarizing and Paraphrasing** This skill is similar to main idea. You may need to summarize to answer questions in writing. When you summarize, you tell what happened without all the details. When you paraphrase, you say things in your own words.

Here is a test question from an article about sloths in this unit. See if you can answer it.

Sloths may vary from about 16 to 29 inches long. This makes them about the size of a ______.

A guinea pig

B mouse

C medium-sized dog

D deer

To answer this question, you have to draw on your prior knowledge. Think about the sizes of the four animals named. Then picture a ruler 12 inches long. Sixteen inches is four inches more than a ruler. Which one of the four animals could be from 16 to 29 inches? You know that a mouse and a guinea pig are small, and a deer is a large animal. Those facts are your prior knowledge. Only a dog could be from 16 to 29 inches long. So the only possible answer is C.

Main Idea

Objectives 1.E.4.a, b, f, g; 2.A.3.a; 2.A.4.c, d, e; 2.A.6.e; 3.A.6.a

Everything you read is *about* something. Think of the last book you read. You could probably describe in one or two sentences what it was about—even if it was a long book. It's the same with each chapter in the book. It's even the same with individual paragraphs. Each one has a **main idea,** the idea that the paragraph is about.

In many paragraphs, there is one sentence that expresses the most important idea. It is called the **topic sentence.** It is usually the first or last sentence of the paragraph. But it could be any sentence. The other sentences in a paragraph support the topic sentence. Some paragraphs do not have a topic sentence, just details.

- Main idea questions usually ask you to choose the best summary of the main idea. A summary will state the main idea in a different way. Look for the answer that tells what the entire selection or paragraph is about, not just the details.
- Some main idea questions ask you to choose a title for the selection or for part of the selection.

Guided Practice

Read this folktale of the Saora people of India. Then answer the questions that follow.

Long ago, people had tails. They were very proud of them. People swished their tails as they walked. They went along sweeping the ground behind them.

This was fine as long as there were few people. But as the number of humans increased, a problem developed. People kept tripping each other by stepping on their tails. There were constant groans, yells, and thuds as people fell to the ground.

One day, the god Kittung visited a crowded market. As he walked along, someone stepped on his tail. Down he went in a heap, falling against a stone and chipping two teeth. The people around him roared with laughter.

Angrily, Kittung pulled off his tail and threw it aside. Seeing what the god had done, all the other tails got scared. They broke away from their owners and ran away as fast as they could.

Kittung's tail grew into a palm tree. The other tails became blades of tall grass. Someone got the idea of making them into brooms. And so people were able to sweep the ground as they had done when they had tails.

Which of these sentences expresses the main idea of the first paragraph?

- **A** Long ago, people had tails.
- **B** They were very proud of them.
- **C** People swished their tails as they walked.
- **D** They went along sweeping the ground clean behind them.

Choice A, *Long ago, people had tails,* seems to be the main idea of the first paragraph. You should look at the rest of the answer choices before deciding, though. Choice B tells about the first sentence, so it is not the correct answer. Choice C and choice D both describe what people did with their tails so they, too, support the first sentence. Thus, choice A is the correct answer.

What is the main idea of the second paragraph of the story?

- **A** This was fine as long as there were very few people.
- **B** But as the number of humans increased, a problem developed.
- **C** People kept tripping each other by stepping on their tails.
- **D** There were constant groans, yells, and thuds as people fell to the ground.

The sentences in choices A, B, and D all support choice C, so it must be the topic sentence. Therefore, choice C is the correct answer.

In the last paragraph, which sentence tells the main idea?

- **A** Kittung's tail grew into a palm tree.
- **B** The other tails became blades of tall grass.
- **C** Someone got the idea of making them into brooms.
- **D** And so people were able to sweep the ground as they had done when they had tails.

Choices A, B, and C all support choice D. So choice D is the correct answer. The three questions on this page all ask for the topic sentence of a paragraph.

Write a title for paragraph 3 of the story. Explain why it is a good title.

____

____

____

____

____

____

Your title should be about the whole paragraph. It should include the main character and give an idea of what happens. You might write "Kittung Falls Down" but that doesn't tell enough about the paragraph. The title "A God Gets Angry" gives a better idea of what happens in the paragraph.

The main idea of this story is to ______.

- **A** warn people against laughing at others' bad luck
- **B** explain how and why people started making brooms
- **C** explain why palm trees are taller than blades of grass
- **D** explain how people are different from animals

Was your answer B? All traditional cultures tell stories like this one. They use such tales to explain events that happened far back beyond people's memories, or things about nature. The last paragraph tells you what this story explains.

Which of these would be the best title for this story?

- **A** "How People Lost Their Tails"
- **B** "How Kittung Lost His Tail"
- **C** "When People Had Tails"
- **D** "Why People Keep the Ground Clean"

Was your answer A? The story not only tells how Kittung lost his tail, but also how people lost their tails. So choice B is wrong. The story also tells about how people used to have tails, but it goes on to tell how they also lost them, so choice C is wrong. Choice D is incorrect because the story doesn't tell why people keep the ground clean. Choosing a title for a story is another way to identify a main idea. Ask yourself, "What is the main thing that happens in this story?"

Read the following notice to parents and answer the questions.

Highland Elementary School

Dear Mrs. Becker:

The fifth grade classes of Highland Elementary School are planning a field trip on Thursday, May 3. We will visit the Beall-Dawson House and the Stonestreet Museum in Rockville. Buses will leave the school at 8:30 a.m. and return by 3 p.m. Bag lunches will be provided by the school cafeteria. There is a fee of $5 for the trip, including lunch.

If you would like your son or daughter to take part in the field trip, complete the permission form below and return it no later than April 13. Please include the $5 fee.

I hereby give permission for son/daughter ______________________ to attend the school field trip on May 3.

______________________________ ______________________

parent/guardian signature date

Spend a Day in the Nineteenth Century

Step back in time to see how people really lived in the 1800s! You will tour the elegant rooms of the historic **Beall-Dawson House** and see beautiful antiques and furniture. Learn what everyday life was like for Upton and Jane Beall and their three daughters. Hear the stories of the Beall and Dawson families.

Then visit **The Stonestreet Museum of 19th Century Medicine** built in 1852. Here you will learn how doctors practiced medicine over 150 years ago. You'll see a real doctor's office. Doctors' instruments and the medicines that were used are all there!

This selection is mainly about ______.

- **A** the Beall-Dawson House
- **B** a field trip for fifth graders
- **C** the Highland School bus schedule
- **D** permission to go on a field trip

Did you choose B? The question asks you what the whole selection is about. The first part gives you details about the trip, and the second part tells about the places students will visit. Answers A and D are only about one part of the selection. So B is the correct answer.

Visitors to the Beall-Dawson House will mainly learn about ______.

- **A** antiques and furniture
- **B** traveling through time
- **C** the three Beall daughters
- **D** a family's life in the 1800s

The first sentence says that visitors will see "how people really lived," and the third sentence talks about "what everyday life was like." The main idea of the paragraph is that visitors will learn about a family's life in the 1800s, so D is the correct choice. Answers A, B, and C give other details of the tour.

What is the main purpose of the Stonestreet Museum? Explain how the displays help visitors understand the purpose of the museum.

____

____

____

____

____

____

The Stonestreet Museum shows visitors what it was like to go to the doctor in the nineteenth century. Seeing the instruments and medicines in a real doctor's office can help visitors understand what people had to go through and how medicine has changed in 150 years.

Test Yourself

Read an article about an unusual statue. Then answer the questions that follow.

In Enterprise, Alabama, there is a statue of a woman. In her upraised hands, she holds—an insect! Her friend is a beetle with a long snout. The statue may be the world's only monument to a pest.

The insect is called the boll weevil. Its only food is the cotton plant. It lays its eggs in cotton bolls. These are the seedpods of the plants, from which cotton thread is made. The larvae hatch in three to five days. They become egg-laying adults in about three weeks. Larvae and adults eat their way through the cotton bolls. They may breed four or five times in a growing season. In a year, they can destroy a farmer's cotton crop.

At one time, cotton was the biggest crop in the southern United States. Many farmers grew nothing but cotton. It was the surest way for them to make money. Then along came the boll weevil. By 1863, it had ruined cotton farming in Mexico. In 1892, it reached the United States. It spread outward at about 70 miles a year. It destroyed cotton crops across the southern states.

In 1915, the boll weevil reached Coffee County, Alabama. At first, the story there was the same as in other places. Farmers were desperate. They had no crops to sell. Enterprise, the county's largest town, was going broke.

Then a local businessman had an idea. His name was H. M. Sessions. He convinced one farmer, C. W. Baston, to grow peanuts instead of cotton. The boll weevil had left Baston deeply in debt. Baston grew 8,000 bushels of peanuts. He was able to pay off what he owed and even save a little money. Other farmers in the county saw that they didn't have to depend on cotton. They bought some of Baston's peanut crop to use as seed.

It was a new idea for the farmers of Coffee County. They didn't have to depend on just one crop. They could make more money by diversifying—planting many crops. Cotton was still an important crop. But the county no longer had to live or die with it.

By 1919, farmers in Coffee County were doing well again. Then another businessman had an idea of his own. Roscoe Owen Fleming wanted to build a monument to the bug that had saved Enterprise. He paid for part of it himself. Other people made up the difference. In December, the Boll Weevil Monument was raised. At first, the statue was holding a fountain over her head. It wasn't until 1949 that an actual boll weevil became part of the monument. Today, the monument is one of Alabama's leading tourist attractions.

1 This article is mainly about ______.

- **A** how the boll weevil almost ruined a town
- **B** how a town fought back against an insect pest
- **C** why there is a monument to an insect in Alabama
- **D** how farmers can do better by growing several different crops

2 Which of these is the topic sentence of the first paragraph?

- **A** In Enterprise, Alabama, there is a statue of a woman.
- **B** In her upraised hands, she holds—an insect!
- **C** Her friend is a beetle with a long snout.
- **D** The statue may be the world's only monument to a pest.

3 A good heading for the second paragraph would be ______.

- **A** Life Cycle of the Boll Weevil
- **B** What a Boll Weevil Eats
- **C** How Cotton Grows
- **D** A Destructive Pest

4 Explain why "boll weevil" is a good name for this insect. Include at least *three* things about the boll weevil in your answer.

____

____

____

____

____

____

5 Which of these is the topic sentence of the fifth paragraph?

A Then a local businessman had an idea.

B He convinced one farmer, C. W. Baston, to grow peanuts instead of cotton.

C Other farmers in the county saw that they didn't have to depend on cotton.

D There is no topic sentence.

6 Which of these would be the *best* title for the whole article?

A "The Bug that Saved Enterprise"

B "Fighting a Destructive Pest"

C "A Most Unusual Monument"

D "A Good Idea for Farmers"

7 How did C. W. Baston become a model for other farmers in Coffee County? Tell *two* ways he helped them.

____

____

____

____

____

____

Details

(**Objectives** 1.E.4.b, g; 2.A.3.a; 2.A.4.d)

You could probably understand a selection by noting the main idea of every paragraph. But you would only have a summary of the main ideas. Good and interesting information comes from **details.** They can help you see, hear, and feel along with a character. Details and facts in a selection provide information that supports the main idea.

Guided Practice

Read this selection. Then answer the questions that follow.

Choi waited nervously in the airport waiting room. He picked up a magazine someone had left. Of course, it was in Korean, as were all the advertisements and signs in the airport. Choi had lived in America since he was two. He could speak Korean, but he could not read it. How was he going to get along in this country? Would he recognize this sister he had never met? Would she recognize him? She was supposed to be wearing a blue dress and a hat with flowers. He saw lots of women dressed in that manner. What if he didn't know Eun Shun when he saw her? What if she couldn't come?

Three months ago, Choi hadn't known that he had a sister. Then his father had seen the notice in the Korean community newspaper in Los Angeles. Looking for family in the United States, it had said. His own name and his father's had popped out. Letters and e-mails had been exchanged, and now, amazingly, he was in Korea.

A woman was approaching him. She was dressed just as Eun Shun had described in the message. She was holding a sign with his name on it in English letters. Choi stood up. The woman was crying. Now he was crying, too, as he hugged his sister.

Where was Choi waiting for his sister?

A in a restaurant

B in an airport

C on a street corner

D in a government office

The correct answer is B. You will find this detail in the first sentence of the selection. Details like this help you picture the scene you are reading about.

How was Choi supposed to recognize his sister?

A by the flowers in her hair

B by a magazine she was carrying

C by a photograph she had sent

D by the clothes she was wearing

The correct answer is D. Paragraph 1 of the selection says, "She was supposed to be wearing a blue dress and a hat with flowers." This tells you that Choi will recognize his sister by the clothes she is wearing.

Which of these statements about Choi is true?

A He could read Korean but not speak it.

B He could speak Korean but not read it.

C He had lived all his life in the United States.

D He hadn't seen Eun Shun since he was two.

You can find this information in paragraph 1 of the selection, too. Sentence 5 specifically says, "He could speak Korean, but he could not read it." So choice B is the correct answer.

Explain how Choi found out that he had a sister. Use details to support your answer.

____

____

____

____

____

The answer to this question is in paragraph 2, sentence 2. Choi's father had seen a notice in a Korean community newspaper in Los Angeles. The ad was from a woman who was looking for family members. Choi's name and his father's name were mentioned.

Read this selection. Answer the questions that follow.

There is a pretty, 1,188-acre lake near Webster, Massachusetts. People come there to relax, to swim, and to go fishing. But mostly, they come to pose for photographs. No, they don't want their pictures taken by the lake. They want them taken beside the sign that announces the name of the lake. And why might that be? Welcome to Lake Chargoggagoggmanchauggagoggchaubunagungamaugg.

That is its real name. On small maps, you may find it as "Lake Webster," but it has been identified by its full name since the 1600s. Of course, the spelling is not always exactly the same. Once, a town sign painter added a few G's.

The lake was named by the Nipmuck Indians. They were the first to fish there. The Narragansett, Pequot, and Mohegan peoples all fished there, too. These tribes did not always get along, but they did respect each other's fishing rights at the lake. Its name means "the fishing place at the boundaries and neutral meeting grounds." In the 1920s, a newspaper reporter wrote about the lake. He said that its name meant, "You fish on your side. I fish on my side. Nobody fish in the middle." Later, he admitted making the story up. But his meaning is still sometimes reported as the true one.

Lake Chargoggagoggmanchauggagoggchaubunagungamaugg is the longest place name in the United States. But it doesn't set a world record. That honor goes to a small town in Wales. Its name is Llanfairpwllgwyngyllgogerychwyrndrobwyllantysiliogogogoch.

What state is Lake Chargoggagogmanchauggagog-gchaubunagungamaugg in?

A New York

B Connecticut

C Maine

D Massachusetts

The answer to this question can be found in the first sentence of paragraph 1, "There is a pretty, 1,188-acre lake near Webster, Massachusetts." So the correct answer is D.

The name of the lake means ______.

A "You fish on your side. I fish on my side. Nobody fish in the middle."

B "the beautiful lake where fish jump out of the water"

C "the fishing place at the boundaries and neutral meeting grounds"

D "the place where we all made peace and had a great feast of fish"

Though the selection mentioned that a reporter said that the name of the lake meant, "You fish on your side. I fish on my side. Nobody fish in the middle," it also states that he later admitted making the story up. In paragraph 3, sentence 5, it states that the lake's name meant "the fishing place at the boundaries and neutral meeting grounds." That would make the correct answer C. In this case, you have to be careful in checking to be sure which is the correct answer.

Llanfairpwllgwyngyllgogerychwyrndrobwyllanty-siliogogogoch is the name of a town in ______.

A Ireland

B Wales

C Thailand

D Mexico

Choice B is the correct answer. Look back to the last paragraph of the selection, sentences 3 and 4, "That honor goes to a small town in Wales. Its name is Llanfairpwllgwyngyl-lgogerychwyrndrobwyllanty-siliogogogoch."

Why do people visit Lake Chargoggagoggmanchaug-gagoggchaubunagungamaugg? Include at least *three* details from the selection in your answer.

____

____

____

____

____

____

Paragraph 1, sentences 2 and 3, can help you answer this question. It says people visit the lake to relax, to swim, and to fish. But most people go to the lake to pose for a picture in front of the sign with the longest place name.

Test Yourself

Read this selection from a mystery, told by a boy named Zach. Then answer the questions that follow.

The brass door handles were polished to a shine. You could see your reflection in them. Amalia was about to push open one of the doors, but a doorman beat her to it. He wore white gloves and a blue uniform with gold shoulder braids. He looked like an army officer from the War of 1812. He waved us in with a sweep of his arm and a broad smile. Amalia thanked him with a nod and a wave of Mom's dark-blue purse. She walked past him briskly. Two steps into the lobby, she stopped dead. She put her finger to her lip.

The hotel was a block long. The lobby was as long as the hotel. People were everywhere, moving, talking, laughing. Finding Spyros here was as likely as spotting him at the ballpark.

"So what do we do now, Nancy Drew?" I said.

Amalia had dropped the grown-up act. She was my 13-year-old sister again. "I don't know," she said. "We could wait by the front desk. Or the elevators? What do you think?"

I looked around. "I don't think we should stay in one place," I said. "It's just too big. Let's walk back and forth slowly."

"Okay," she said doubtfully. "If anyone asks, we'll say we're guests here and we're waiting for our parents to come down."

The lobby had an old-fashioned look. On one side, behind brass railings, stuffed chairs were arranged around tables of dark wood. The floor was carpeted. The design on the carpet showed a forest. Hunters were chasing deer with dogs and old guns shaped like trumpets. On the other side, where the front desk was, the floor was made of polished stone squares. They were black and white, in a chessboard pattern. The place *smelled* old, too. It seemed like the people should be wearing clothes from 100 years ago.

But they weren't. Everyone was dressed like the lawyers in shows on TV. At a tall table, a man in a gray suit was talking loudly into a cell phone. A bored-looking woman in a pink dress sat beside him sipping a drink. That wasn't Spyros. He would be by himself.

"Look for someone who's alone," I whispered. Amalia nodded. A large, bald-headed man sat reading a magazine. He held a metal briefcase in his lap. Could that be Spyros? A man Dad's age with a black-and-white beard sat alone on a couch. He was blind. He wore dark glasses and held a white cane. A younger man was pacing in a small circle near the door of the restaurant. He looked like he was waiting for someone. But he was too nervous to be Spyros.

1 Which of these illustrations shows the doorman at the hotel?

A

B

C

D

2 What was Amalia carrying?

A a black umbrella

B a book

C a bunch of flowers

D a dark-blue purse

3 What was the design on the carpet?

A black and white squares

B a hunting scene in a forest

C an orchestra playing music

D a scene of knights on horseback

4 Explain why Amalia and her brother Zach thought they would have a hard time spotting Spyros. Use at least *three* details from the selection to answer the question.

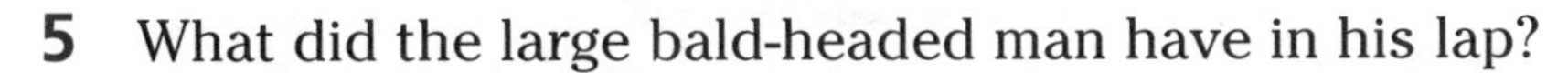

5 What did the large bald-headed man have in his lap?

A a cell phone

B a cane

C a briefcase

D a newspaper

6 Zach describes the lobby as looking old-fashioned. Describe *three* details from the selection that support this statement.

Inferences and Conclusions

Objectives 1.E.4.c, d; 2.A.4.g

A writer does not state every fact plainly. Writers want you to figure out some details based on what you know and what you are reading. This is called **making inferences.**

Jodie heard the old grandfather clock strike three. Now she was wide awake. She turned over, hoping she could go back to sleep.

The story says:
The clock struck three. Jodie wanted to go back to sleep.

You know:
Most people sleep at night.

You can infer:
It is 3 a.m., not 3 p.m.

When you put pieces of information together, you are **drawing conclusions** or **making generalizations.**

I put on my boots first. Then I tried to put Mac's leash on, but he kept running in circles. His tail was going a mile a minute. A gust of wind blew the door open, and Mac ran out. "Stop, Mac!" I cried. But Mac didn't get very far. He was up to his nose in snow.

The story says:
Mac's tail is wagging.
Mac is running in circles.
Mac runs out the door.
There is deep snow on the ground.

You know:
Dogs move when they are excited.

You can conclude:
Mac wants to play in the snow.

Guided Practice

Read this story, told by a girl named Eva. Then answer the questions that follow.

I was out working in the fields that morning. The yellow sun was halfway up the sky. The red sun was just rising, turning the light orange. I remember thinking how pretty that time of day was when suddenly I heard the whine of an Arrowhead. I looked up and saw it coming in low over the horizon. It seemed almost close enough to touch as it flew directly over my head toward the base.

I was already running. The regular shuttle from Earth wasn't due for a month. I could never remember a starship making an unscheduled call. But there it was—a bright green Arrowhead!

Where does this story take place?

____

____

____

____

____

____

The story never says that Eva is on another planet. But it does mention the "shuttle from Earth." From this you can infer that the story takes place on a planet other than Earth.

An "Arrowhead" is *most likely* a ______.

A small spaceship from Earth

B flying car used on Eva's planet

C spaceship that travels between stars

D weapon fired by an enemy

The selection states that the Arrowhead is headed toward a base, so it is coming from another planet. Eva says, "The regular shuttle from Earth was not due for a month." That suggests that the Arrowhead is coming from Earth, but is smaller than a regular shuttle. There is enough information for you to conclude that choice A is the correct answer. But there is no information to support choices B, C, and D.

Read the next paragraph of Eva's story. Then answer the questions that follow.

I realized something else. This visit was a surprise to Dad and the council, too. Otherwise he would have said something about it. Who could be visiting the colony? And did it mean good news or bad? One thing sure, I wouldn't be in the dark for long. As I came over the hill, the Arrowhead was coasting to a stop on the landing strip. People were pouring out of the dome to greet it. I could see Dad's green jacket.

Eva suggests that the visit of this starship is ______.

- **A** something to be afraid of
- **B** very out of the ordinary
- **C** a good thing for her family
- **D** a shuttle that arrives every month

In the second sentence Eva says that the Arrowhead's arrival was a "surprise." This should lead to the conclusion that such an event does not happen every month or regularly (choice D). Eva doesn't seem to be afraid (choice A) or to think this is good for her family (choice C). Since everyone comes out to see the Arrowhead, you can conclude that its arrival is out of the ordinary (choice B).

Which of the following conclusions can you draw from this story?

- **A** Eva and her family are not human.
- **B** Eva's dad is one of the leaders of their colony.
- **C** Food for the colony has to be brought in from Earth.
- **D** Earth people have to wear spacesuits to survive on this planet.

When you read questions like these, ask yourself: Are there any reasons for drawing one conclusion rather than another? In this case, there are no reasons to think Eva is not human (choice A) or that the narrator needs a spacesuit (choice D). Eva is working in a field, probably growing food, so choice C is not right. That leaves choice B. Eva suggests that she will find out quickly what's happening—most likely from her father. If he is being given information before other people, chances are he is a leader of the colony. Thus, choice B is correct.

Read this advertisement for a music concert. Then answer the questions that follow.

Which of these is a conclusion you can draw from the advertisement?

A The concert will be cancelled if it rains.

B It is less expensive to buy a ticket the day of the concert.

C Area motels and campgrounds will be crowded during the concert.

D The concert will not feature country music.

Even though the concert is outdoors, the selection doesn't say anything about the concert being cancelled or postponed for rain. So choice A is incorrect. The ad does list ticket prices, but it is more expensive to buy a ticket at the door. So choice B doesn't work either. The music being performed is shown at the top and bottom of the ad. Choice D cannot be right because country music is listed. The ad says that camping on theater grounds will not be allowed. So you can conclude that the area motels and campgrounds might be full during the two-day event.

About how many bands will be playing during the two-day concert? Explain how you came to your conclusion using facts from the advertisement.

____

____

____

____

____

____

The advertisement gives you enough information to make a good guess about how many bands will perform. The concert has 5 stages with new performances every hour between 9 a.m. and 6 p.m. That is about 45 bands per day for a total of 90 bands over the two days.

Where would you *most likely* find this advertisement?

A in a grocery store

B at a record store

C at a car dealer

D in a monthly magazine

Although this advertisement could be placed anywhere, you can conclude that the *best* answer is choice B. Since most people who go to music stores enjoy music, the advertisement would get the most attention there.

Why do you think recording devices are not allowed at the concert? Give at least *two* reasons to support your answer.

____

____

____

____

____

____

Most concerts do not allow recording devices because the performers don't want people recording their music and selling the copies. They want fans to buy their albums. In addition, the concert promoters may not want you to bring cameras or recording devices because they could get stolen or destroyed. They don't want to be responsible for your valuables.

Test Yourself

Read an article about a spy. Then answer the questions.

Lydia Darragh

Lydia Barrington was born in Ireland. At the age of 24, she married William Darragh, a teacher. Soon afterward, the young couple moved to colonial Philadelphia. Lydia worked as a nurse. She tended patients in their homes. She became well known as a midwife, helping women who were having babies. She also had several children of her own. In the Revolutionary War, one of her sons was a young officer in George Washington's army.

During the Revolutionary War, British soldiers captured Philadelphia and were staying in that city. As it happened, General William Howe made his headquarters near Lydia Darragh's home. General Howe was the leader of all the British soldiers in the city. General Howe angered the people of Philadelphia by forcing them to let British officers sleep and eat in their homes. But Lydia Darragh made the best of it. She listened all the time, picking up bits of information about British army plans. She took notes in code. She had a small group of trusted messengers who worked for her. When the chance came, her friends would take the messages to Darragh's son, Charles.

This went on for several weeks. Then Lydia's own family was ordered to let a British officer live in their house. This man was General Howe's top assistant. One evening, this same man told Lydia's family to go to their rooms early. He needed her back room for a private meeting. Other British officers arrived at Lydia's house. Lydia Darragh just pretended to go to bed. She then hid outside the door where the officers were meeting and listened. She heard them planning a surprise attack on General Washington's camp. Lydia crept back to her room. When her "guest" knocked on the door to tell her that the officers were leaving, she acted like he had awakened her from a deep sleep.

The next day, Darragh told her family she was going to buy flour at a nearby mill. She asked General Howe for a pass to show the British guards. Once past them, she hurried toward the American camp. She met an officer she knew and gave him the information. He took the message directly to George Washington.

Back home, Lydia waited for news. The British troops marched out of Philadelphia. They soon returned. Washington had somehow learned of their plans, and he was ready for them. For a time, the British officer living in their home suspected the Darragh family. But he never suspected Lydia. She had been sound asleep the night of their meeting.

1 You can guess that Lydia Barrington Darragh was probably born about ______.

A 1700

B 1730

C 1770

D 1800

2 Which of these *most likely* explains how Lydia started picking up information about British army plans?

A British officers told her, thinking she was on their side.

B She listened at windows to private meetings.

C She overheard people talking while she was on her nursing calls.

D She got into General Howe's headquarters and read his private papers.

3 Which of these is a conclusion you can draw from the article?

A Lydia Darragh became a spy only after a British officer was put up in her home.

B Lydia's husband and children knew she was working as a spy.

C George Washington's camp was not many miles outside the city of Philadelphia.

D After the events described in this passage, Lydia stopped working as a spy.

4 Which of these best explains why the word "guest" in the third paragraph is in quotation marks?

A Lydia Darragh spoke the word.

B The officer was not really an invited guest.

C The author is using the word in an unusual way.

D "The Guest" is the title of the passage.

5 What do you think would have happened if Lydia Darragh's message had not gotten through? Explain your answer using details from the selection.

____

____

____

____

____

____

6 Explain why Lydia Darragh can be called a spy. Give at least *two* examples from the selection to support your answer.

____

____

____

____

____

____

Making Predictions

(Objectives 1.E.2.c; 1.E.4.e; 3.A.8.b)

Do you realize that you think ahead while you read? Suppose you start to read a book called *Laptop Detectives* in which three kids find a laptop computer. You can probably predict from the word "detective" in the title that they will get into some trouble with the laptop. If you are reading a book about Thomas Jefferson, you can guess or predict that there will be something in the book about the Declaration of Independence. You make that prediction based on what you know: that Jefferson wrote the Declaration.

When you try to look ahead to what's going to happen, you are **predicting.** The events or happenings you predict are called **outcomes.** A good prediction combines the clues found in the story with your own prior knowledge. **Making predictions** keeps your mind moving forward as you read.

Guided Practice

Read this story about going west in 1849. Then answer the questions that follow.

Gone to See the Elephant

The old mountain man called himself Tinch. He looked doubtfully at Uncle Jess's map. "Well, I won't say this wouldn't get you to Sacramento," he said. "But I won't say it would. I don't know who this Pierce Walker is. But I do know he's never been to California. Not by this route, he hasn't. And this shortcut of his is no shortcut."

"What are you talking about, mister?" Uncle Jess looked challengingly at Tinch. "You calling Mr. Pierce Walker a liar?"

"Never met him," Tinch said. "And I've known just about every man what's crossed the Sierra Nevada since old Jed Smith back in '26. This route of his takes you straight across the desert. Your shortcut means 700 miles without being sure of finding water. Better go the long way around by Fort Hall."

"Sure, and everyone else will get to the gold fields before us," Uncle Jess snorted. He snatched the map back. "The race goes to the swift, friend! You get nowhere in life if you don't take risks!"

"You're taking another risk with those horses." Tinch waved at Uncle Jess's fine team. "It's none of my business, but they'll never make it over the passes. If I were you, I would sell them. Go with oxen. They are slow, but they will hold up better." But Uncle Jess was walking away.

Seeing the elephant is an old expression that means "coming up against something that's too big to handle." You can predict that this story will mostly be about ______.

- **A** going to see a frontier circus
- **B** conflict between Tinch and Uncle Jess
- **C** a dangerous journey by wagon
- **D** wildlife on the plains of the West

This selection is the beginning of a longer story. The title "Gone to See the Elephant" suggests it is about something that is too big to handle easily. Choice B has already happened, so it cannot be predicted. Uncle Jess and Tinch disagreed about the map. There is no reason to think either choice A or choice D will be a main part of the story. You can see that the story will focus on getting to California, and Tinch has already predicted trouble if Uncle Jess doesn't follow his advice. So, choice C is the best answer.

What will Uncle Jess probably choose to do?

- **A** take the shortcut and keep his horses
- **B** take the shortcut but use oxen
- **C** go the long way and keep his horses
- **D** go the long way but use oxen

The story suggests that Uncle Jess wants to get to California to beat the gold rush. You can tell from the story that he is impatient. He challenges Tinch, "snorts" at his suggestions, and walks away. He probably will want to take the shortest route and use horses. So, the best choice is A.

Uncle Jess and the people with him will most likely ______.

A hire Tinch as a guide

B never make it to California

C get to California quickly by the shortcut

D get to California after much hardship

Tinch predicts hardships, and he knows the area. So, it's a good prediction that it will not be an easy trip. Most likely, Uncle Jess will not "hire Tinch" (choice A), since Tinch wants to go a different way. The story tells you that the shortcut is across a dangerous desert. So, it will not be quick. That leaves out choice C. The trip will be hard. However, the story seems to be told by someone who was with Uncle Jess. It thus seems likely that at least someone will get to California (choice D), sooner or later.

What do you think will be the outcome of this story? Give at least *two* reasons to support your answer.

____

____

____

____

____

____

Although the story doesn't say, it is a good prediction that Uncle Jess and his group will arrive in California after a long and difficult trip. Because of Uncle Jess's impatience, the party will probably have an exhausting trip. But his determination suggests that they will make it to California.

Now read part of an article about an author. Answer the questions that follow.

Word Wizardry

Good books don't happen by magic—not even books about magic. You can't wave a wand and make a book appear. It takes an idea, lonely time, and a lot of hard work to write one. But the end results can seem like magic. Just ask Joanne K. Rowling.

Joanne's idea came to her when she was traveling by train from Manchester to London, England. Later, she would say that it "just fell into my head." The idea was a story about a boy who was a wizard and didn't know it. The story would tell about his adventures at a wizard school. At first, that was all Joanne knew.

It was a hard time for Joanne Rowling. She had a baby that she was raising by herself. She was a teacher, but just then she had no job. She had always dreamed of being a published author. She had started two adult novels but never finished them. She had never thought of writing for or about children. "Children's books chose me," she later explained.

Soon she had a name for her boy wizard. But it would be five years before the world would know the name of Harry Potter. First would come the lonely time and hard work.

Today, Rowling's books have been published in 200 countries and 55 languages. They have all received enthusiastic reviews from her readers. In fact, kids stand in long lines to get the latest book. They can't wait to find out the plot. Rowling said she could never have predicted the success of the books. Each of the five "Harry Potter" books has been on bestseller lists and won numerous awards.

You can predict from this beginning that "Word Wizardry" will mostly be about ______.

A how authors get their ideas

B how an author did research to write a book about magic

C how to become a best-selling author

D how the "Harry Potter" books, about a boy who is a wizard, were written

These few paragraphs are the beginning of a longer article. You know that it will most likely be about books and writing books. However, you can see in advance that the article will deal with the Harry Potter books, written by Joanne Rowling. So, choice D is correct. Even if you have not read these books, you can see that the selection is probably going to talk about them, and not about writing in general (choices A and C) or about doing research.

What do you think the next part of paragraph four could be about?

A how Joanne Rowling's life changed after she became famous

B what the next Harry Potter book will be about

C how Joanne Rowling will help young writers

D how Joanne Rowling wrote her first book

The first paragraph of the article clues you to the fact that it will be about writing a book. The third sentence tells you it is a "lonely time and a lot of hard work." Choice D is the best answer since the passage focuses mostly on writing. Choices A, B, and C are all about the future.

How do you think the public will respond to future books written by J. K. Rowling? Use details from the selection to support your answer.

____

____

____

____

____

____

The last paragraph tells about the success of J. K. Rowling's books. Based on the fact that her books have been published in many countries, kids wait in long lines to buy new books, and the books have been on bestseller lists, you can predict that future books will be just as successful.

What will probably happen to J. K. Rowling's books twenty years from now?

A Kids won't want to read them anymore.

B Kids will continue to read the books.

C The books won't be printed anymore.

D Libraries will throw out the books.

You may know that the "Harry Potter" books have been made into movies. Because the books and movies have been so successful, it is a good prediction that kids will still be reading the books many years from now. So, choice B is correct.

Test Yourself

Read the following article. Then answer the questions that follow.

In an average year, about 8,000 Americans are bitten by rattlesnakes. How many do you think die from their bites? No, not that many. Guess again. No, better lower your guess some more. The correct number is eight to 15.

The rattlesnake is dangerous, all right. But it's not as deadly as most people think. In about half of all rattlesnake bites, the snake injects very little venom or none at all. Venom is a poison that certain snakes and insects can inject into humans or other animals. One fourth of all rattlesnake bites cause painful swelling but are not threatening to life. The other fourth are the dangerous ones. People can die if they don't get a medicine called *antivenin.* Usually, they do get the medicine. That's because of the 75 animal-poison centers around the country. They provide antivenin to hospitals. They also give out information on how to treat the bites of rattlesnakes and other poisonous animals.

Animal venom is still largely a mystery to science. The more a person or animal weighs, the more venom is needed to cause death. This means it would take more snake venom to kill a deer than a wolf. But you can't tell how much venom a rattlesnake injects when it bites. (Snakes don't use measuring spoons.) So you never know how much antivenin is needed. And venoms of different animals act in different ways. Some attack the heart or the muscles. Some poison the blood or the nerves. Some attack more than one body system. And venoms may contain more than 130 different chemicals. Doctors don't yet know how many of them work.

What they do know is that many animals aren't as deadly as people think. Take the black widow spider, for instance. Its bite is painful but rarely dangerous. Doctors advise people to wash the bite, put ice on it, and take an anti-swelling medicine, such as aspirin. The same goes for tarantulas. Their fangs look nasty. But for most people, their bite is no worse than a bee sting. That is also the case with most scorpion stings.

But watch out for the brown recluse spider and the bark scorpion! Both these creatures live in the deserts of the southwest part of the United States. Anybody who is bitten by one of these two insects should get to a hospital at once. But even these deadly creatures aren't as feared as they used to be. The state of Arizona used to record about two deaths per year from bark scorpion stings. Since 1965, there has not been a single one.

This is *not* to say that it's a good idea to pick up a scorpion! Safety and common sense are still the best protection against animal venom. In other words, if you are careful, the chances are you will not be bitten by a scorpion or snake. As for rattlesnakes, you wouldn't want to keep one for a pet. But let's not forget all the rats and mice they eat! Even a rattlesnake has its place in the environment.

1 A person bitten by a rattlesnake would *most likely* ______.

2 The person *most likely* to die from a rattlesnake bite is one who ______.

A is bitten by a very large snake

B has been bitten previously

C was playing with the snake

D lives far away from a hospital

3 Which of these statements would you *not* be able to predict from the article?

A More people will learn that most scorpions and spiders are not dangerous.

B Science will learn more about animal venom and how to treat it.

C Deaths from snakebite and scorpion stings will continue to go down.

D Scientists will develop an antivenin that works against all animal venoms.

4 Of the following predictions, which one is accurate based on the article?

A If all the rattlesnakes were removed from a ranch, the number of rats and mice would increase.

B A person who was bitten by a tarantula would probably not need help because there would be no pain.

C If an adult and a child were both bitten by a dangerous animal or insect, only the child would get sick.

D A person who goes walking in a desert in the Southwest would likely get bitten by a bark scorpion.

5 Based on the article, which of the following is a good prediction for the year 2010?

A The number of people who die from rattlesnake bites will rise.

B The brown recluse spider will become extinct within ten years.

C National Parks will give hikers antivenin to carry with them.

D There will be more animal-poison centers in the United States.

6 What would probably happen if you kept a rattlesnake as a pet? Give reasons from the article to explain your answer.

____

____

____

____

____

____

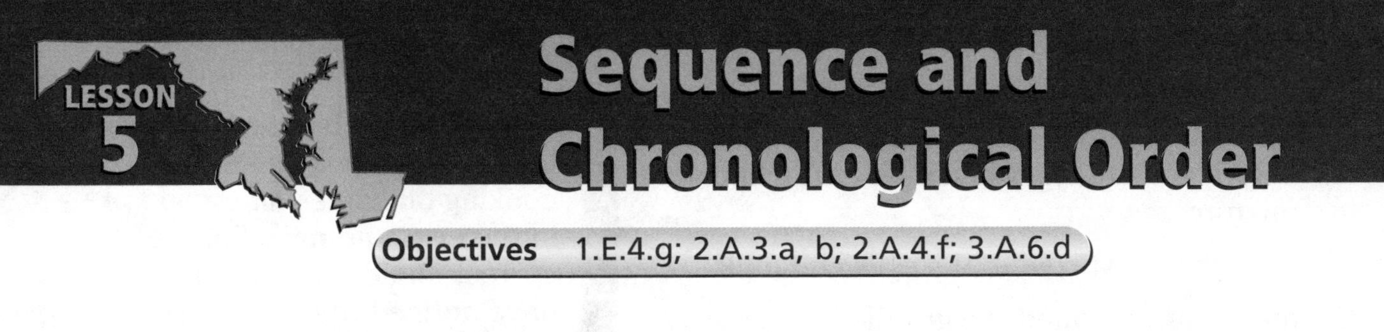

Sequence and Chronological Order

Objectives 1.E.4.g; 2.A.3.a, b; 2.A.4.f; 3.A.6.d

In your life things happen in order.

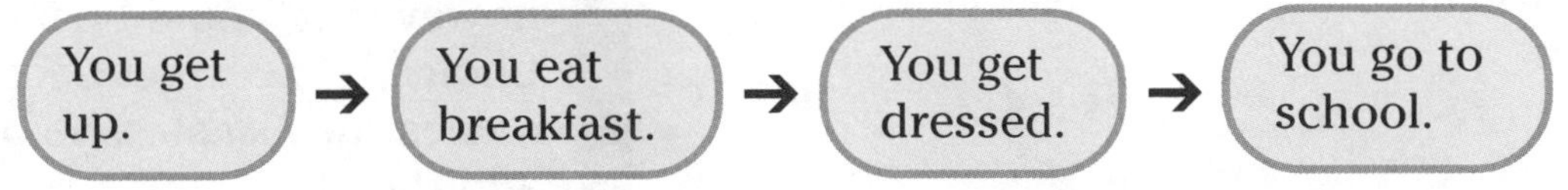

The order in which things happen is called **sequence**. When you read, you need to follow the sequence of events. Whether you are reading about someone's life, the steps of a science experiment, or a story, you need to follow the sequence of events.

Stories are not always written in sequence. An author may begin by telling you about something that happened last week then go back to an event two weeks earlier. You can follow the sequence of the story by looking for clues. Watch for dates and time words; they are good clues to sequence. Some words are also clues to the sequence of events.

Look for *sequence* words	
first	recently
second	earlier
third	later
last	finally
next	now
before	after
following	then

Guided Practice

Read this recipe. Then answer the questions that follow.

Healthier Pancakes

Mix together 2 cups whole-wheat flour with one-half cup wheat germ and two teaspoons baking powder in a bowl. Stir in 1 tablespoon brown sugar and 1 teaspoon salt. Mix well.

In another bowl, beat two large eggs lightly. Combine with $2\frac{1}{2}$ cups fresh milk. Add this liquid to the flour mixture. Stir batter well to get out lumps. Then stir in 2 tablespoons cooking oil.

Next, heat a griddle. It should be hot enough that sprinkled drops of water sizzle on it. Use a large spoon to pour spoonfuls of the pancake batter on the griddle. Turn once when bubbles form on the surface of the pancakes and pop. Take the pancakes off the griddle when their edges are slightly dry.

2 c. whole-wheat flour	1 tsp. salt
$\frac{1}{2}$ c. wheat germ	2 large eggs
2 tsp. baking powder	$2\frac{1}{2}$ c. milk
1 tbsp. brown sugar	2 tbsp. cooking oil

According to this recipe, you add the cooking oil ______.

A before you add eggs and milk to the flour mixture

B after you've stirred in the eggs and milk

C after you've heated the griddle

D after you add the brown sugar and salt

In paragraph 2, the word *then* tells you that stirring in the cooking oil comes *after* you stir in the eggs and milk. So, the correct choice is B. You may have noticed that choice D is also true. On a reading test, however, it would be incorrect. Choice B is correct because it names the *last* step before you add the oil.

Which of these steps does the recipe ask you to do *first?*

A Stir in salt and brown sugar.

B Watch for bubbles to form on the surface.

C Stir to get out the lumps.

D Mix flour, wheat germ, and baking powder.

A recipe explains the steps of cooking something in just the right order or sequence. There is a first step which must be done before the others. The first step in this pancake recipe is mixing, as stated in choice D. The steps mentioned in the other choices come later. Choice D is correct.

After you heat the griddle, which of these steps does the recipe ask you to do *third?*

A Very carefully turn the pancakes over.

B Take the pancakes off the griddle when their edges are slightly dry.

C Watch for bubbles to form on the surface of the pancakes.

D Spoon pancake batter onto the griddle.

The last paragraph describes how to cook the pancakes on the griddle. The first step is to spoon out the pancake batter onto the griddle (choice D). You can figure out that the next step is to keep an eye on the pancakes as they cook and watch for bubbles (choice C). The third step is to flip or turn the pancakes (choice A). This is the correct choice. Only after these steps, should you take the finished pancakes off the griddle (choice B).

What are *two* things that you need to do before pouring spoonfuls of pancake batter on the griddle? Explain your answer using details from the selection.

____

____

____

____

____

Paragraphs 1 and 2 tell you how to make the pancake batter. Paragraph 3 tells you what to do before pouring the batter onto the griddle. First you must heat the griddle. Then to make sure it is hot enough, you sprinkle a few drops of water onto the griddle. If they sizzle, the griddle is ready for the batter.

Read this selection, narrated by a girl named Loni. Answer the questions that follow.

As soon as I got home, I threw myself into a hot bath to cool off. If it hadn't been the worst day of my life, it was pretty close. First, I missed the school bus after my alarm clock didn't go off. I had to run to Stone Boulevard to catch the city bus. I was still late for school. Then I discovered that I had forgotten my math homework. It was on my desk at home. When I told Ms. Padilla, she looked at me like I'd said the dog ate it or something.

After school I had soccer practice. I was a step or two behind the whole time. I missed a couple of passes, and Coach Barone yelled at me. It was almost dark when I left the field. I got to the bus stop just in time to see the bus pull away. It seemed like forever, but finally another bus came. And, of course, I had to stand for the whole ride home. As I came up the stairs to our apartment, I could hear the TV in the living room. Good, I thought. No one will want to talk to me.

Look for these *sequence* words

after	then
finally	first

Loni discovered that she had forgotten her math homework when she ______.

- **A** threw herself in the bathtub
- **B** finished soccer practice
- **C** got to the bus stop
- **D** ran up the stairs

From the selection you know that Loni ran up the stairs (choice D) and took a bath (choice A) at the end of the day so both answers don't make sense. The selection tells you that she had to run to Stone Boulevard to catch the bus. *Then* she discovered that she had forgotten her math, so she must have been at the bus stop. Choice C is correct.

Which of these events was the last one to happen *before* Loni got into the bath?

A Her alarm clock didn't go off.

B Her soccer coach yelled at her.

C She heard the TV in her apartment.

D She waited for a bus in the dark.

This question asks what was the last thing that happened *before* Loni got into the bath. Even though all the events mentioned in the choices happened before the bath, the *last* one is when Loni heard the TV in her apartment, choice C. She believed that her family would be watching TV, and she would have a chance to be alone and relax after a hard day. Choice C is correct.

What is one thing that did *not* happen *after* soccer practice?

A Loni took a hot bath.

B Loni missed the bus a second time.

C She heard the TV in her apartment.

D Coach Barone yelled at Loni.

From the selection, you know that Loni missed the bus going home from practice, heard the TV in her apartment, and took a hot bath. These events all happened *after* soccer practice. The only one that did not happen after practice is choice D. Coach Barone yelled at Loni *during* soccer practice.

What did Loni do *after* she missed the school bus and *before* she arrived late at school? Explain your answer.

____

____

____

____

____

Paragraph 1 tells you what happened when Loni missed the school bus. She had to run to Stone Boulevard to catch the city bus. But this still made her late for school.

Test Yourself

Read the next selection about an inventor. Then answer the questions.

The Real McCoy

Elijah McCoy was born near Colchester, Canada, in 1844. His parents once were slaves in Kentucky. In 1837, they escaped. They made their way north and became farmers.

As a boy, Elijah McCoy showed an interest in machines. He could take them apart and put them back together. When he was 16, his parents sent him to school in Scotland. He returned to Canada as a "master mechanic and engineer." But he could only find work as a laborer. McCoy thought he might have a better chance in the United States. In 1865, he moved from Canada to Detroit, Michigan. But there, too, he could not find work as an engineer. He got a job as a fireman and oiler on the Michigan Central Railroad.

It was the age of steam-powered trains. Moving parts had to be coated often with oil. That was part of McCoy's job. Every few miles, the train had to stop so he could oil it.

McCoy thought about this problem. Then in 1872, he invented an "oil cup" for steam engines. It dripped oil by itself when and where the oil was needed. There was no need to stop the train. The invention was a huge success. It was soon being used on railroads everywhere. Later it was used in ships, factory machines, and drills. Other people copied this invention. But most users wanted the original. They would ask for "the real McCoy."

Over the next 50 years, Elijah McCoy patented dozens of inventions. In 1916 he designed a new oiling machine. It was needed to oil the new "superheater" trains. Four years later, he started his own company. But in 1923, McCoy was badly injured in an automobile accident. He never fully recovered. Six years later, he died.

Later, steam was replaced by other sources of power. Many of McCoy's inventions were no longer needed. But two of them are still widely used today. In 1874, McCoy's wife, Mary, was complaining about how hard it was to iron clothes on a table. Elijah's response was to invent the ironing board. Almost 25 years later, Elijah McCoy was watering his lawn with a hose. There ought to be a faster and easier way to do this, he thought. There wasn't. So he invented one—the lawn sprinkler. People still remember his name, too. When something is genuine and original, we still call it "the real McCoy."

1 Which of these events happened *first* in McCoy's life?

A McCoy began to work for the Michigan Central Railroad.

B McCoy went to school in Scotland.

C McCoy invented the oil cup.

D McCoy moved to Detroit, Michigan.

2 Which of these did McCoy invent *last?*

A the oil cup

B the oiling machine

C the ironing board

D the lawn sprinkler

3 McCoy started his own company ______.

A after he invented the oiling machine

B before he invented the oiling machine

C after he was injured in an automobile accident

D after other sources of power had replaced steam

4 In what year did Elijah McCoy make his *first* important invention?

A 1865

B 1874

C 1916

D 1872

5 For how many years did Elijah McCoy live in the United States? Explain how you know from the selection.

____

____

____

____

____

____

6 What did Elijah McCoy invent *after* the ironing board but *before* the oiling machine? Explain how you know using details from the selection.

____

____

____

____

____

____

LESSON 6

Prior Knowledge

Objectives 1.E.2.d; 1.E.4.h; 2.A.4.f, j; 3.A.6.e, f

Your mind is busy when you read. You may not be aware of it, but you are always **applying prior knowledge.** That means thinking about things you already know that can help you understand what you are reading.

Suppose you start reading an article about dinosaurs. You may know a lot about dinosaurs. You may have seen pictures of them. Maybe you've seen some bones in a museum. You may know when they lived and the reasons scientists think they died out. You know the names of several kinds of dinosaurs and a few facts about them. These things all help you understand what you are reading.

As you read, ask yourself questions such as: What do I know about this topic? What do the title and the pictures make me think of? Then use this knowledge as you read.

Guided Practice

Read this selection now. Use what you know to answer the questions that follow.

Sloth is an old word that means "laziness." It is also the name of a group of slow-moving mammals. Sloths live in the forests of Central and South America. There are several kinds. They vary from about 16 to 29 inches long. They are covered with short grayish-brown hair.

Sloths live all their lives hanging upside down in trees. They eat, sleep, and give birth this way. They come down to the ground only about once a week. In trees, they move very slowly, one leg at a time. On the ground, they can barely crawl.

Sloths sleep with their heads between their front legs. To animals that hunt them, they look like the stumps of tree branches. A simple plant called green algae grows in the hair of some species. It looks like leaves and moss. This gives the sloth even more protection.

Sloths are a group of slow-moving mammals. Which of these animals are mammals?

A frogs, toads, salamanders

B snakes, lizards, crocodiles

C slugs, snails, turtles

D elephants, pigs, cats

You know that mammals are warm-blooded animals that feed on their mothers' milk when young. The animals in choice A are all cold-blooded animals. The same is true of the animals in choice B. The animals named in choice C are slow moving, like sloths, but they are not animals that feed on their mothers' milk when young. So choice D is the correct answer.

Sloths live in Central and South America. What are some countries in which they may live?

A Costa Rica, Venezuela, Brazil

B India, Thailand, Vietnam

C England, France, Spain

D Egypt, Jordan, Iraq

You know something about different regions of the world and the countries in each of them. The countries in choice A seem to be all in Central and South America, but let's look at the other answer choices, too. Choice B, India, Thailand, Vietnam are countries in Asia. Choice C lists countries that are in Europe, and the countries in choice D are in the Middle East. So choice A is the correct answer.

If you didn't know the answer to the last question, you could find it by looking in a ______.

A world atlas

B dictionary

C wildlife encyclopedia

D book about sloths

A world atlas is a book of maps for places around the world. So that is most likely the correct answer. You also know that a dictionary is where you would look up words you don't know. A wildlife encyclopedia would not tell you about countries, and neither would a book about sloths. So choice A is the correct answer.

The color of the sloth's hair and the green algae that grows in the hair help the sloth to ______.

A hang onto the tree branches

B hide from its enemies

C stay warm in the rain forests

D swing from tree to tree

The color of the sloth's hair and what grows in it would not help a sloth hang onto the tree branches. So choice A is wrong. Those things could help a sloth hide from its enemies, so choice B could be correct but let's finish looking at the rest of the choices. Choice C, stay warm in the rain forests, is wrong because rain forests are already warm and there's no need to keep warm. Also, the gray hair and green algae would not serve that purpose anyway. Swing from tree to tree, choice D, is also wrong because the gray hair and green algae would not help the sloth do that. So choice B is correct.

What is another animal that is about the same size as a sloth? Explain how you figured out your answer.

____

____

____

____

____

____

The selection tells you that sloths may vary from 16 to 29 inches long. You know how long an inch is. A ruler is usually 12 inches long. You can use that knowledge to picture a sloth in your mind and compare it to other animals you know. A medium-sized dog or a raccoon is about the size of a sloth.

Now read this letter. Answer the questions that follow.

3309 Hasselback St.
Annapolis, MD 21401
August 2, 2004

Dear Torin,

Well we're here. It was a boring three-day drive, but I did get to play a lot of video games in the car. I can see sailboats in the bay from my grandparents' backyard. Tomorrow we are supposed to tour the United States Naval Academy. We are going to see the Naval Museum and the crypt of John Paul Jones. Today, we walked all around Annapolis to see the historic sights. Boy, are my feet sore! I've been eating lots of seafood, too. Crab cakes are now my new favorite food. Grandpa promised to take me on a sailing cruise on the Chesapeake Bay before I leave. I'll have lots more to tell you about. See you when school starts.

Your friend,

Alejandro

In the first line of the heading, the abbreviation *St.* stands for ______.

- **A** Station
- **B** State
- **C** Saint
- **D** Street

You know that a letter includes the sender's address and that the abbreviation *St.* in an address usually stands for *Street.* Choice A, *Station,* can be true, but *Street* is still the more likely answer. Choice B, *State,* doesn't really make sense here and neither does choice C, *Saint.* So choice D is the correct answer.

Alejandro wrote his letter from ______.

A Museum

B Maryland

C Marley

D Malaysia

You know that the second line of a heading includes the city and state the person is writing from. You can look there for the answer. *Malaysia* is the name of a country, but the city name *Annapolis* that comes before *MD* tells you that *MD* is an abbreviation for a state. Only choice B, Maryland, is the name of a state. It is the correct answer.

What caused Alejandro's feet to be sore?

A he had blisters

B he stood during the cruise

C he did a lot of walking

D he sat in the car for too long

Alejandro said he spent a lot of time walking all around Annapolis. You know that sometimes your feet hurt when you've done a lot of walking. The letter doesn't say anything about Alejandro getting blisters on his feet. So the correct answer is C.

Why has Alejandro decided that crab cakes are his new favorite food? Give at least *two* reasons for your answer.

____

____

____

____

____

____

Alejandro tells his friend that he has been eating a lot of seafood. Maryland is known for its seafood because many places in the state are located on the shore where seafood is caught fresh. You may know that Maryland is especially known for its crabs, and Annapolis has many fine restaurants. So it is no wonder that crab cakes are now Alejandro's favorite food.

Test Yourself

Read this article about an unusual family trip. Then answer the questions that follow.

How I Spent My Summer Vacation

by Julie Gradison, with Frank Maltesi

My mom started a new job this fall. She is a college teacher, and she was hired by the University of South Dakota. We had to move from Charlottesville, Virginia, to Vermillion, South Dakota. Dad is a photographer. He always says he could live and work anywhere. Still, he wasn't very happy about the move, until he figured out how to make it an adventure.

Mom and Dad met on a mountain-bike trip. My brother Erik and I were both on two wheels before we learned to read. Our family vacations usually involve bicycles. One year, we biked through Shenandoah National Park. Another time, we toured battlefields of the Civil War. But those were both pretty close to home. At first, when Dad said, "Let's bike to South Dakota," Mom said, "That's 1,500 miles!" Then she said, "Let's do it!"

Actually, it turned out to be 1,714 miles, give or take a block or two. It took us 58 days, counting time off for rest and sightseeing. We couldn't take the shortest route, no, not us. See, it's history that Mom teaches. She likes our adventures to be educational. The first part of our trip took us along the old pioneer route into Kentucky. That's the trail Daniel Boone blazed. For the last part, we followed the Missouri River from St. Louis. That was the route of Lewis and Clark's famous trek, when President Thomas Jefferson sent them to explore and map the West. A lot of people like to travel their route. Some people we met were following it all the way to Oregon. Of course, most of them were in cars. Some were trying to do at least part of the trip by boat. We were the only ones on bikes.

The first few days were the hardest. We had to climb the Blue Ridge Mountains. There were days that first week when I could hardly get out of bed. Then it was mostly downhill all the way to St. Louis, Missouri. The last third of the trip was mostly uphill again. But by then, we were in shape for it. We rode tandem bikes, so Mom and Dad did most of the work. But we sure looked forward to a cool shower and a comfortable bed at the end of each day. And you wouldn't believe how much we ate!

Was it fun? That's not exactly the word I would use. I feel proud for having done it. But I don't look forward to doing it again any time soon. Dad is talking about a West Coast bike trip next summer. I'll agree, if the only biking we do is from a rented cottage to the beach.

1 Julie Gradison's family biked from Virginia to South Dakota. That means they traveled mostly ______.

- **A** north to south
- **B** south to north
- **C** west to east
- **D** east to west

2 Look at this map. Which letter shows the state where Julie's mom got her new job?

A **B** **C** **D**

3 Where would you expect to read an article like this?

- **A** a book of short stories
- **B** a book about history
- **C** a magazine
- **D** an encyclopedia

4 Julie says "you wouldn't believe how much we ate!" Explain why the family was so hungry. Use examples from the article and your own prior knowledge.

____

____

____

____

____

____

5 The family may take a West Coast bike trip. Which of these states is on the West Coast?

A Alabama

B West Virginia

C Wyoming

D California

6 Explain why it was hard for the author to get out of bed during the first week. Give at least *two* reasons for your answer.

____

____

____

____

____

____

Summarizing and Paraphrasing

Objectives 1.E.4.f, g; 2.A.2.c, d; 2.A.4.d; 2.A.6.c

You know how to find the main idea of a selection. You know how to distinguish between details that support the main idea and those that are less important. Sometimes it helps to be able to **paraphrase** the main idea of a selection in your own words. When you explain all the important events and details, you're **summarizing** the selection.

How would you summarize your weekend when describing it to a friend? How would you choose what was most important?

Guided Practice

Read a student's letter to a newspaper. Then answer the questions that follow.

I'm a fifth-grade student at Banneker Elementary School. Your article about Greenwood Park Zoo raising its admission prices has prompted my very first letter to a newspaper. Look, I love the zoo. I know it takes money to keep animals healthy, pay the staff, and build things like the new gorilla habitat. But I have some ideas that the zoo might consider instead of higher ticket prices.

First, charge a separate fee for special exhibits. For instance, last year everyone wanted to see Rani, the baby elephant. Why not charge another dollar or two to view popular animals like Rani?

Another idea is to raise prices for extras. The zoo could keep admission the same but charge more to ride the Safari Train or have lunch at the Zoofeteria.

Finally, why not start an adopt-an-animal program? Most kids would give part of their allowance money to help support an animal. There could be a scale—five dollars for a lizard, say, up to a lot for a baby elephant. There could be special rates for families or school classes. You could have your picture taken with the animal you adopt.

I'm no expert. I don't know if these ideas would work. I'm just asking the zoo to "think creatively" before raising admission prices.

Sincerely,

Kayla Brocker

Which paragraph does *not* contain any facts that would be included in a summary of the letter?

A paragraph 2

B paragraph 3

C paragraph 4

D paragraph 5

The main idea of the letter is that Kayla is suggesting ways for the zoo to raise money instead of raising admission prices. This idea is expressed in the first paragraph. The next three paragraphs contain details that support it. The last paragraph does not support the main idea. It is only a conclusion that restates it. So D is the correct answer.

Which details would be included in a summary of paragraph 4?

A Why not start an adopt-an-animal program? You could have your picture taken with the animal you adopt.

B Why not start an adopt-an-animal program? Kids would give money to help support an animal.

C You'd have to give a lot to support a baby elephant. There could be special rates for families or school classes.

D There could be a scale for the different animals. You could have your picture taken with the animal you adopt.

The main idea of this paragraph is what Kayla is suggesting—an adopt-an-animal program. This point must be included in a summary. The most important supporting detail is how the program would work—kids would give money. The other details are related to the main idea, but are not needed for understanding it. The answer is B.

Summarize the letter. Include the main idea and only the most important details.

____

____

____

____

____

____

A student suggests ways the zoo can raise money without raising admission prices: charge a separate fee for special exhibits, raise prices for attractions other than viewing animals, and start an adopt-an-animal program.

Now read a news item and answer the questions that follow.

WASHINGTON— A panel appointed by the president has warned that the world's oceans are in trouble.

"We have major problems," one of the panel's scientists said. At least one third of the fish species commonly caught for food are "overfished." Some of the larger ones, such as tuna, have dropped 90 percent over the last 50 years. Half of the world's people live near an ocean. Pollution from the land starves fish of oxygen, leaving "dead zones" in offshore waters. One such zone in the Gulf of Mexico is as big as New Jersey. Non-native species brought in by ships drive out native species and damage ocean habitats.

In addition, a decline in one species can cause an environment to crash. For instance, the sea otter population in Alaska's waters has dropped by about 85 percent since the mid-1980s. This has caused a huge increase in sea urchins, the otters' favorite food. The sea urchins in turn eat the seaweed that is a habitat for other animals.

"The oceans are in trouble," commented one member of the president's panel. The only disagreements seem to be on how bad the problem is and what people should be doing to reverse it.

Which of these is *not* a detail that belongs in a summary of the selection?

A Many food fish species are "overfished."

B Half the world's people live near an ocean.

C Pollution from land leaves "dead zones" in the ocean.

D Ocean habitats are being damaged.

The main idea of this selection is a warning that the oceans are in trouble. Details naming the kinds of trouble support the main idea. They include overfishing, pollution, and habitat damage. The fact that half the world's people live near an ocean may explain the pollution, but it is not required in a summary. The correct answer is B.

Which of these ideas from the third paragraph belongs in a summary of the selection?

A A decline in a single species can damage an environment.

B Alaska's sea otter population has dropped by 85 percent.

C Sea urchins are the otters' favorite food.

D Sea urchins eat the seaweed that is the habitat for other animals.

Paraphrase the last paragraph.

____

____

____

____

____

____

A detail in a summary has to support the main idea. The most important detail of the third paragraph is how ocean environments can be damaged. The rest of the paragraph describes an example of that detail: how a decline in a single species (in this case, the sea otter) can damage an environment. That's why A is the correct answer.

Test Yourself

Now read a folktale from Africa and answer the questions that follow.

Long ago, before people ruled the earth, animals could talk to each other. Back then, Spider, Deer, and Leopard were the best of friends. Now, Spider had a famous vegetable garden. He grew lettuce, sweet potatoes, carrots, and onions. He was also a fine cook. Often he would invite his friends Deer and Leopard over to dine on vegetable stew.

One day, Spider was out digging in his garden when he noticed that a head of lettuce was missing. A few days later, he saw that a whole row of carrots was gone. "Somebody has been stealing my vegetables," Spider complained to Deer. "You're a clever fellow. Tell me what I can do to catch this thief."

Now it happened that Deer himself was the thief. He had been stealing from Spider's garden for some time. Now he knew he had gotten too greedy and was in danger of being caught. "Here is what you should do," Deer said. "Dig a pit in your garden. Build a fire in the pit and let it burn down to hot coals. Then cover the pit with damp leaves. When the thief comes, he'll fall in and you can catch him."

Spider thought it was a fine plan. At once he set about digging the pit. Meanwhile, Deer went to Leopard's house. "Our friend Spider is up to something," he said to Leopard. "He says he wants us to come to his house at midnight. I think he's planning a surprise feast for you."

"Isn't that just like Spider!" Leopard thought. And that night at midnight, he went strolling through Spider's garden toward his house. He fell right into the trap. Hot coals burned his tawny coat. His screams woke Spider, who came running. "What kind of trick is this?" cried Leopard. "Please, help me out before I burn to death!"

"It's no more than you deserve," said Spider. "You fell right into my trap, you thief!" But he helped Leopard out of the pit anyway.

"Why do you call me a thief?" Leopard said. "And why did Deer tell me you were preparing a surprise feast? Look at me! Now my beautiful yellow coat is covered with dark spots!"

Of course, it didn't take long for the truth to come out. And so their fine friendship ended. From that day to this, Leopard has had a spotted coat. And because of Deer's deceiving ways, leopards no longer eat vegetables. Instead they hunt and eat deer.

1 Which of these ideas would you *not* include in a summary of the first paragraph?

A Spider, Deer, and Leopard were the best of friends.

B Spider had a famous vegetable garden.

C He grew lettuce, sweet potatoes, carrots, and onions.

D Often he would cook dinner for Deer and Leopard.

2 Which of these details would be most important to include in a summary of the story?

A Long ago, animals could talk to each other.

B Deer had been stealing from Spider's garden for some time.

C Deer told Leopard that Spider was planning a surprise feast.

D Because of Deer's deceiving ways, leopards hunt and eat deer.

3 What was Deer's plan to keep from being caught? Write a summary of the plan in no more than *three* sentences.

____

____

____

____

____

____

4 Which details *best* summarize what happened to Leopard?

A He fell into the pit and burned his coat. It didn't take long for the truth to come out. But Leopard has had a spotted coat ever since.

B He went strolling through Spider's garden. He fell right into the trap. His screams woke Spider, who came running.

C "Isn't that just like Spider!" Leopard thought. He fell in and burned his coat. Spider called him a thief but helped him out anyway.

D He fell right into the trap. It didn't take long for the truth to come out. And so their fine friendship ended.

5 Paraphrase the main idea of the folktale.

____

____

____

____

____

____

Unit 3: Reading Informational Text

There are two kinds of things to read—literature and information. Most of the reading you do is for information. Informational text can be nonfiction—just what you are reading now. It can also be functional. Functional reading includes information in different forms—recipes, directions, charts, posters, schedules, and even the computer screen. In this unit, you will learn ways to get information from nonfiction and functional text in these seven lessons.

1. **Features of Print** If all printed material were just straight type, you would have a hard time following it. Features of print such as heads, underlines, italic type, and different fonts help you sort out the text.
2. **Cause and Effect** If you don't do your homework [cause], your grades will go down [effect]. To understand an article you will often need to look back for causes or figure them out. This lesson will show you how to find causes and effects.
3. **Problem and Solution** When you solve a problem, you have found the solution. In this lesson you will learn how to identify the problem and the solution in nonfiction.
4. **Comparison and Contrast** Like cause and effect and problem and solution, comparison and contrast is a way that nonfiction reading is sometimes organized. This lesson will show you how to figure out how things or ideas in a reading selection are alike [comparison] and different [contrast].
5. **Author's Purpose and Audience** Why did the author write the article you are reading? Did the author write it for you or for a different kind of reader? You will learn to recognize an author's purpose for writing.
6. **Fact and Opinion** Another part of understanding an author's purpose—and an important part of reading nonfiction—is recognizing when an author is giving an opinion instead of straight facts.
7. **Analyzing Language** To understand all the other informational reading skills, you need to know how to analyze the language an author is using.

Here is a test question from this unit. Even though you haven't read the selection, see if you can answer the question.

In which of these sentences does the author give an opinion?

A Winter has arrived.

B Snow is all over the school playground.

C But no one is happy at recess.

D Snowball fights are not allowed.

This question asks you about the author's opinion. You should be able to pick out the one answer that cannot be proved to be factual. Look at choice C. It says *"No one* is happy at recess." It would be pretty hard to prove that, although the other choices could be proved. So choice C must be the correct answer.

Features of Print

Objectives 1.E.2.a; 2.A.1.a, b; 2.A.2.a, b, c, d, f

When you read, there are things to notice other than words. An indented line, for instance, indicates a new paragraph. That tells you to look out for a new topic with a new main idea. Quotation marks may enclose a speaker's exact words. Or, they may indicate a title or that the words are being used in an unusual way. These are examples of **features of print.** They help you organize your thoughts and understand better what you're reading.

Underlining is one way to make words stand out.

Another is the use of *italics, like this.*

Words ALL IN CAPITALS or in **large bold print** make you pay attention.

Some forms of writing may attract your eye by varying the color or the size of print.

Print in different styles, or *fonts,* may be used for contrast. This is a **serif font.** Some of the letters have thin small lines, called serifs, to finish off their main strokes.

This is a **sans-serif** font. Letters in this style of type have no serifs.

Guided Practice

Read this article about dogs. Note the features of print. Answer the questions that follow.

Chesapeake Bay Retriever

"Hetty is a pet," says her owner, 10-year-old Will Connough. "She's never hunted in her life. But we keep her on a leash in the park, or she'd go straight into the duck pond. You can't stop her from going after anything in water."

Hetty is a Chesapeake Bay Retriever. Any "chessie" owner knows they make good pets. But a chessie is also a born hunting dog.

As a Pet

A Chesapeake Bay Retriever is a sturdy, medium-sized dog with a thick, short, slightly wavy coat. It's a friendly, loyal, and affectionate animal. It sheds in the spring, so it should be brushed daily. It requires regular exercise and loves to run and swim. But as Will Connough knows, it must be supervised carefully.

A Sporting Dog

The breed's special talent is to swim out and bring back waterfowl that have been shot by hunters. It often must swim against heavy winds and tides. It likes cold water and can even break ice. Its oily, woolly undercoat helps it stay warm. It has a powerful neck and chest. But it will carry a wounded duck gently in its jaws.

History of the Breed

Two Newfoundland puppies brought to Maryland by George Law were the ancestors of all Chesapeake Bay Retrievers. "Sailor" and "Canton" were cross-bred with other dogs trained as retrievers. Tales of their offspring's hunting ability were legendary by 1845. The "chessie" became a recognized breed in 1877.

"Chessie" Facts and Figures

Height at shoulder	
male:	23-26 in (58-66 cm)
female:	21-24 in (53-61 cm)
Weight	
male:	65-80 lb (29-36 kg)
female:	55-70 lb (25-32 kg)
Color	brown, sedge (tan) or deadgrass (straw)
Classification	sporting dog
First Bred	United States, 1807

Which of these does the author use to make topic headings stand out?

A italics

B underlining

C large, bold type

D all capitals

Look at the headings. They are not in italics, large, bold type or all capitals. But they are underlined. So choice B is the correct answer.

The word "chessie" is set in quotation marks because ______.

- **A** it's a word spoken by Will Connough
- **B** it's part of the title
- **C** it's translated from another language
- **D** it's a nickname for Chesapeake Bay Retriever

You know that quotation marks can be used for different purposes. "Chessie" is not spoken by anyone. It is not part of a title. There's no suggestion that it's a translation. But it's a pretty obvious nickname for a Chesapeake Bay Retriever. So D is the correct choice.

Basic facts and figures about the Chesapeake Bay Retriever stand out because they are set ______.

- **A** in a table, and in a different font
- **B** in a table, and in several colors
- **C** in a box in large, bold type
- **D** in italics, and in a different font

The "Facts and Figures" are easy to notice. They are arranged in a table. And they use a different type font from the rest of the text. So choice A is the correct answer.

What features of print are used in the title of the article? Explain how they make the title stand out.

____

____

____

____

____

____

The title is centered over the article, and it is larger than the body of the article so you notice it first. It uses both italics and large, bold type and a different font in a different color. That makes it easy to read.

Now read part of a restaurant menu and answer the questions that follow.

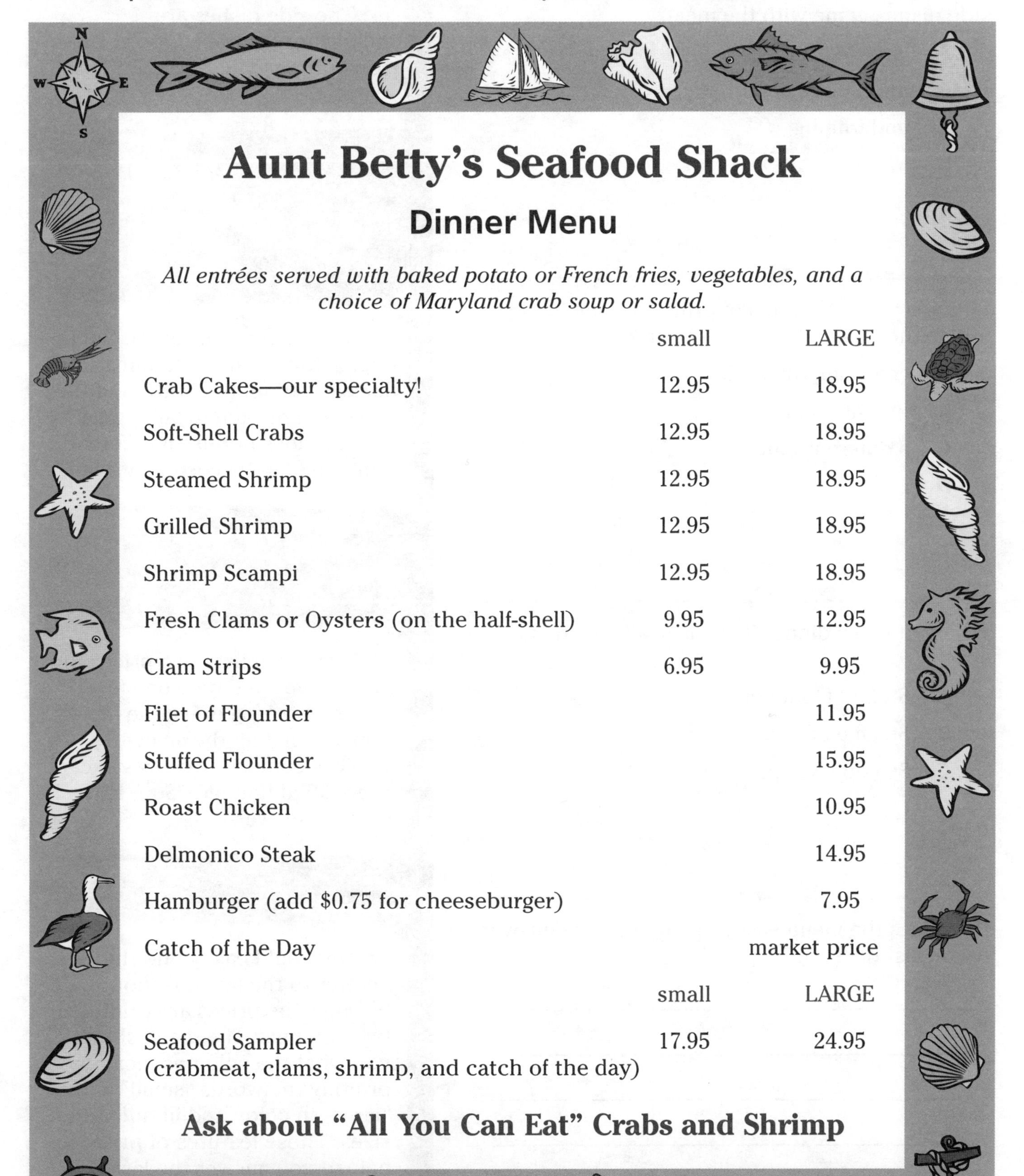

Aunt Betty's Seafood Shack

Dinner Menu

All entrées served with baked potato or French fries, vegetables, and a choice of Maryland crab soup or salad.

	small	LARGE
Crab Cakes—our specialty!	12.95	18.95
Soft-Shell Crabs	12.95	18.95
Steamed Shrimp	12.95	18.95
Grilled Shrimp	12.95	18.95
Shrimp Scampi	12.95	18.95
Fresh Clams or Oysters (on the half-shell)	9.95	12.95
Clam Strips	6.95	9.95
Filet of Flounder		11.95
Stuffed Flounder		15.95
Roast Chicken		10.95
Delmonico Steak		14.95
Hamburger (add $0.75 for cheeseburger)		7.95
Catch of the Day		market price

	small	LARGE
Seafood Sampler (crabmeat, clams, shrimp, and catch of the day)	17.95	24.95

Ask about "All You Can Eat" Crabs and Shrimp

Which of these features of print shows you what side dishes come with the meal?

- **A** large, dark type
- **B** quotation marks
- **C** underlining
- **D** italics

The side dishes are highlighted in italic type at the top of the menu. So choice D is correct.

Which of these features of print does *not* help you notice the "all-you-can-eat" special?

- **A** centering the type
- **B** quotation marks
- **C** a different font
- **D** color

The all-you-can-eat special is highlighted in quotation marks. It is centered on the bottom of the page and printed in large green type. It does not use a different font. So C is the correct answer.

Which of these dinner items is available in only one size?

- **A** Stuffed Flounder
- **B** Steamed Shrimp
- **C** Seafood Sampler
- **D** Clam Strips

The menu lists two prices for some items and only one for others. Looking down the menu, you see that all the answer choices come in two sizes except the stuffed flounder. So A is the correct answer.

How does the menu easily let you find the answer to the last question?

____

____

____

____

____

____

You could easily find the answer to the last question because the prices are printed in two columns. The menu shows you what the columns mean by printing the words "small" and "large" in color, and in different sizes. Those features of print helped you answer the last question.

Test Yourself

Now read this application form and answer the questions that follow.

Annual Fifth-Grade Essay Contest

"Memories of Madison"

What? Write a 500-word essay on your most memorable experiences at Madison Elementary School. Fill out the form below and submit it to your teacher with the essay.

Who? Open to all fifth-grade students.

How? The essay may be written by hand or on a computer. *All essays must be original. Entries not written entirely by the student will be disqualified.*

When? All entries are due Tuesday, April 30. *No exceptions.* Winners will be announced at the graduation assembly, Friday, June 14.

What Can I Win? Three winning essays will be selected. The winners will receive passes for themselves and their families to Water World amusement park. Winning essays will be published in the Bryant County *Times.*

- -

Student's Name ____

Address ____________________________________ Zip ____________

Phone _______________ e-mail address _________________ Teacher ___________

I have been a student at Madison since the ______ grade.

I certify that my essay is original work and that I have received no help in preparing or writing it.

Student's signature ____

I give my permission for my child's essay and photograph to be published in the Bryant County *Times.*

Parent or guardian's signature ______________________________________

Phone _______________

1 "Memories of Madison" is in quotation marks to show that ______.

A someone is speaking

B it is the title of the contest

C the contest isn't really about memories

D words are being used in an unusual way

2 Contest information is organized by headings printed in ______.

A large bold print

B italics

C all capitals

D a different font

3 The part of the application to be filled out by a parent is in ______.

A large bold print

B italics

C a different font

D a different color

4 Which kind of information uses both italics and underlining?

A title of the contest

B subject of the essay

C warnings about rules

D instructions to parents

5 Explain how italics and underlining help you use the form.

____

____

____

____

____

____

6 Suppose you entered the essay contest. Tell at least *three* ways you could use features of print to highlight your essay.

____

____

____

____

____

____

Cause and Effect

Objectives 2.A.1.a, b; 2.A.3.a, b; 2.A.4.f

When you read, you probably see connections between ideas and events. These connections explain why things happen. Your reading makes more sense when you understand these *why* connections. Look for clue words that signal **cause and effect.** The thing that happens is the **effect.** The reason it happens, or what made it happen, is the **cause.**

Cause

These clue words signal causes:

because, since, reason for,
due to, on account of

Effect

These clue words signal effects:

then, so, led to, as a result

If there are no clue words, you may need to draw a conclusion. Ask yourself "why did this event happen?" (the cause) and "what happened because of the event?" (the effect). It might help to mentally add your own clue word ("because" or "so").

Guided Practice

Read this article about weather. Answer the questions that follow.

Lightning is electricity. It's like the spark you get from rubbing a wool sweater on a dry day. It's a lot bigger, of course. But like that tiny spark, lightning happens because of a build-up of electricity in the air. This build-up may take place between two rain clouds. Or, it may happen between a rain cloud and the ground. Scientists do not understand why rain clouds produce high-power electricity. But when they do, lightning appears. In fact, the air itself carries the electricity we call lightning. Lightning travels along a path of air, which acts something like a wire. The lightning heats the air to a temperature of about 18,000°F in just a few millionths of a second. This rapid heating causes the air to burst outward, as in an explosion. As this wave of suddenly superheated air travels outward from the lightning bolt, it produces the sound we call thunder.

Look for *cause-and-effect* words:

because	then
since	so
reason for	led to
due to	as a result
on account of	therefore

Lightning is caused by ______.

A a build-up of electricity

B air that becomes very hot

C airplanes passing through a cloud

D an explosion in the sky

Lightning is the effect. What is its cause? The article states that lightning happens because electricity builds up. Notice the word *because* in that sentence. That's a signal that a statement of the cause follows. So choice A is correct.

A wave of suddenly superheated air travels outward from a lightning bolt. As a result ______.

- **A** clouds change color
- **B** the sound of thunder is produced
- **C** it lights up the sky
- **D** the air changes to water

Here the phrase *as a result* tells you that you're looking for an effect. The cause is "a wave of suddenly superheated air." What effect does this lead to, according to the article? The final sentence in the article states that the heating of the air produces the sound of thunder (choice B), which is correct. *Produces* is the clue word that points to the effect. Choice C is an effect of lightning, not of air. Choices A and D are not connected to the cause.

Lightning strikes the ground because ______.

- **A** it's a large spark of electricity
- **B** it heats the air to a high temperature
- **C** the air carries it between a rain cloud and the ground
- **D** the air carries it between two rain clouds

Here the effect is lightning striking the ground. There is no clue word that points directly to the effect. But there are clues just the same. Lightning may happen between a rain cloud and the ground. Lightning travels along a path of air. This chain of clues leads you to the correct answer, choice C. None of the other choices are connected to the effect.

Explain what causes the air to burst outward.

____

____

____

____

____

____

The article states "This rapid heating causes the air to burst outward, as in an explosion." So your answer should be something like "Rapid heating, caused by lightning causes the air to burst outward."

Now read this set of directions and answer the questions that follow.

Painting Your Treehouse

Now that you've built your treehouse, paint it! Paint will make it look better and protect the wood from rain and sun.

First, carefully measure the surfaces you want to paint. Calculate the total area in square feet so that the helpful person at the hardware store or home center will know how much paint you'll need.

Preparing the Wood

A good paint job requires preparation. Don't try to paint rough or dirty wood, as it will make the paint peel, crack, or wrinkle. Scrub the surface well with soap and water. Remove any old, loose paint with a wire brush. Sand the rough spots. All this takes some work, but it will make the paint stick better.

Choosing the Right Paint

Use latex paint. It washes easily off brushes and paint-spattered hands with soap and water. You can thin it with water instead of paint thinner, which gives off dangerous fumes and can easily catch fire. Latex paint also dries quickly. Don't use it directly on redwood or red cedar, as these woods contain chemicals that can stain the paint. Applying a coat of primer first should prevent staining. Unlike oil-based paints, you can apply latex to a damp surface.

Using the Brush

All paint is a mixture of solids and liquids that separate in the can. For that reason, paint should be mixed thoroughly before applying. So that you can do the job quickly, use brushes at least three inches wide. Nylon-bristle brushes work best with latex paint. Dip the brush only a little way into the paint so that hardened paint does not build up in the heel. Paint only with the end of the bristles. Reverse the brush often.

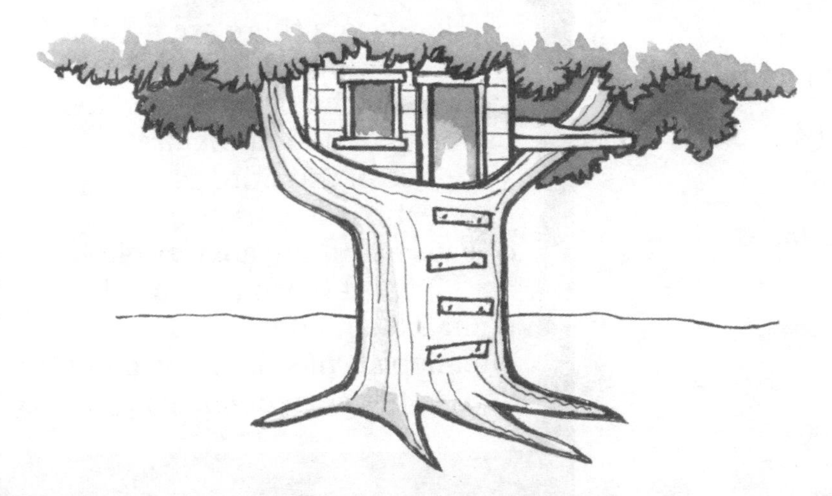

Look for *cause-and-effect* words:

because	then
since	so
reason for	led to
due to	as a result
on account of	therefore

Because paint will separate in the can ______.

- **A** it is a mixture of solids and liquids
- **B** you should use nylon-bristle brushes
- **C** old paint should never be used
- **D** it should be mixed before applying

The word *because* clues you that paint separating in the can is the cause of your taking some action. The action you take is the effect. The clue words *for that reason* in the last paragraph point to the correct answer, choice D: Mix the paint. Choice A is a cause of the paint separating, not an effect. Choices B and C are not related to the cause.

One thing you can do to make paint stick better is to ______.

- **A** use latex paint
- **B** use brushes at least three inches wide
- **C** scrub the surface well
- **D** protect the wood from rain and sun

The effect is "to make paint stick better." No clue words point to the cause. But the whole third paragraph is about this subject. It gives several suggestions for making paint stick better, including "Scrub the surface well with soap and water." So choice C is the correct answer. Choice D is an effect, not a cause, of making paint stick better, while choices A and B have nothing to do with the effect.

Which of these is *not* a reason the article gives for using latex paint?

- **A** You don't need to use paint thinner.
- **B** It's easier to clean up afterward.
- **C** Chemicals in wood won't stain it.
- **D** You can apply it to a damp surface.

Here again there are no clue words that point directly to the cause. But the effect, "Use latex paint," is stated in the first sentence of the third paragraph. The rest of the paragraph is a list of causes. All the answer choices are given as reasons to use latex paint except choice C. Those chemicals *will* stain latex paint. So C is the correct answer.

According to the article, what will happen if you dip the brush deeply into the paint?

____

____

____

____

____

Here you need to remember why the author tells you to "dip your brush only a little way into the paint." The clue words *so that* point to the effect you *don't* want: Hardened paint will build up on the heel of the brush.

Test Yourself

Read this article about a student's science project and answer the questions that follow.

My science teacher, Mr. Soriano, had a cool way of teaching us about motion and forces. He had us work in teams to design and build Rube Goldberg machines.

Now, you may wonder what a Rube Goldberg machine is. Rube Goldberg was a newspaper cartoonist who died in 1970. He used to draw these crazy machines. They would use a complicated series of steps to do a simple task, like swatting a fly or wiping a window. It was his way of making fun of technology.

Mr. Soriano showed us some of Goldberg's cartoons. Then he gave us our assignment. We had to invent something that used at least three simple machines to perform a task. We had to set it up so that each machine would trigger the next. My team chose a balloon popper since we thought it would be easy to make. Other choices, like the card flipper or the tack picker-upper, seemed too tricky.

We started by rolling a marble down a ramp made from a cardboard tube. It gained speed. At the bottom, it hit a wooden ruler that was fastened at the middle to a tower of blocks. The force of the marble's impact made the ruler swing like a lever. The upper end bumped a toy train car. As a result the car was propelled down a sloping track. At the bottom, a golf ball was balanced on a tee. The car knocked the ball off onto a clothespin. Due to the weight of the ball, the clothespin opened, releasing a string. It was wound around a set of pulleys. As they turned, the other end of the string came down. A magnet was glued to it. The magnet picked up a metal bar. This released another lever made from a piece of a kid's building set. At the other end of this lever was a pencil with a pin through the eraser. When it moved up, it popped the balloon.

It was even more complicated to build than to describe. We had to test some steps over and over to make them work. (Mr. Soriano said that's how new machines are engineered in the real world, but it was still annoying.) For instance, take that first step. At first we couldn't get the marble to hit the lever hard enough to bump the train car. That was because it didn't have enough energy as it came down the ramp. We solved that by making the ramp steeper.

Rube Goldberg designed his machines to make people laugh. Ours actually worked—about one time out of every three. Each time, it took us about ten minutes to set it up again. But it was fun.

1 Why did Mr. Soriano have the class build Rube Goldberg machines?

A to teach them about Rube Goldberg's work

B to teach them about motion and forces

C to teach them how real machines are made

D because it would be fun

2 Explain what caused the lever to move up to pop the balloon.

____

____

____

____

____

____

3 The string holding the magnet was released because ______.

A a magnet was glued to one end

B the magnet picked up a metal bar

C it was wound around a series of pulleys

D the golf ball opened the clothespin

4 Because the students didn't make the ramp steep enough ______.

A the marble did not hit the lever

B the lever did not bump the train car

C the marble did not roll all the way down

D the golf ball was not heavy enough

5 A toy train car was propelled down a sloping track. What was this movement an *effect* of? What was it the *cause* of?

____

____

____

____

____

____

LESSON 3

Problem and Solution

Objectives 2.A.1.a, b; 2.A.3.a

Sometimes when you read, you are looking for a solution to a problem. You need to be able to identify a solution and to match it with the problem it's intended to solve. Suppose you're growing a vegetable garden. Your spinach leaves are turning black and dying. You consult a gardening book. You have to find the exact problem and note the solution. Otherwise, you may end up putting out snail poison when all your spinach needs is a certain plant food added to the soil.

Problem

Solution

Guided Practice

Read these instructions for a computer game. Then answer the questions that follow.

Troubleshooting

If you have a problem with *Mars Mission,* please try the following:

First read the "ReadMe" document that came with your game. It was written after this manual went to the printer. It may contain extra information about possible problems.

If you have installed the program but it fails to open, restart your computer.

If the screen freezes or animation is slow, your computer probably has out-of-date software. That is the cause of most technical problems. Colossal Games cannot fix it. Please check the Web sites of the makers of your computer and its parts. New software may be available.

- If this doesn't help, check the support system of our Web site at http://www.colossalgames.com. See if an upgrade is available for your game. This may solve the problem.
- If everything else fails, try our Technical Support line at 1-800-555-4321. Be prepared to give the name of the game and the exact nature of the problem. For example, what exactly was on the screen when the problem occurred? What were you doing? If there was an error message, what did it say? Does the problem happen every time?

If the program won't open, the manual suggests that you ______.

A get new software

B check the company's Web site

C restart the computer

D call the Technical Support line

You've followed the instructions to install the program. But it won't start when you click on it. That's the problem. It's described in the third paragraph of the instructions. That paragraph then states the solution: restart your computer. So C is the correct answer.

The company tells you to check their Web site for an upgrade if ______.

A new software doesn't solve the problem

B you can't get help from Technical Support

C you have trouble installing the software

D you have the wrong kind of computer

Here you're given a solution and asked to identify the problem it can solve. There's no point in going to the company's Web site if you don't need the upgrade. The phrase "If this doesn't help" points back to the problem as stated in the last paragraph: You may need to get up-to-date software for your computer. So A is the correct answer.

For any problem, the quickest solution may be found ______.

A by calling the Technical Support line

B at the company's Web site

C by buying a different copy of the game

D in the "ReadMe" document

Any one of these suggestions may solve your problem. But the first paragraph of the instructions tells you to try the "ReadMe" document first. It may offer the solution to your problem. So D is the correct answer.

The animation moves in a slow, jerky manner. Explain how the directions suggest a solution to this problem.

____

____

____

____

____

The instructions state that if animation is slow, the problem is out-of-date software in your computer. They advise you to "check the Web sites of the makers of your computer and its parts. New software may be available." So "install new software" is the solution.

Now read this news item and answer the questions that follow.

Spirit Camera Back at Work

NASA has announced that the camera on the Mars rover Spirit is up and running again.

A new picture from Spirit was successfully taken and returned to Earth Wednesday. The camera on the costly Mars mission had been sending back only meaningless data for more than a week. NASA engineers hope to have it fully back on line by this weekend.

Engineers guessed that Spirit's "flash memory" was overloaded. The flash memory works something like the memory card in a digital camera. It was filled with data gathered during the flight from Earth and in its first few days on Mars. The engineers got it working again by erasing the flash memory by remote control.

What was the problem with the Mars rover Spirit?

A Its computers had stopped working.

B A rough landing had broken its camera.

C It cost too much money to fix.

D Its camera had stopped sending pictures.

The first paragraph tells you that the problem was with the camera. But you have to read the second paragraph to know just what it was. The camera was not broken. It was still working, but it was "sending back only meaningless data." So D is the correct answer.

How did engineers solve the problem?

A They erased the camera's flash memory.

B They used an ordinary digital camera.

C They used data gathered during the flight from Earth.

D They sent a Shuttle crew to repair the camera.

The problem was with the camera. The solution was what the engineers did to get it working. The last sentence tells how they did it: by erasing the camera's flash memory. So A is the correct answer.

How did the engineers know that the problem had been solved? Explain both the problem and the result of the engineers' solution.

____

____

____

____

____

____

The engineers knew there was a problem because the camera was sending back "meaningless data." They could tell they had solved it when "A new picture from Spirit was successfully taken and returned to Earth." So your answer should be something like, "The camera took and sent back a picture."

Test Yourself

Read the following biography of an African American leader. Then answer the questions that follow.

Frederick Baily was born into slavery in Maryland in 1818. As a child, he was sent to work in Baltimore in the home of Sophia Auld. She often read aloud from the Bible. Frederick asked her to teach him to read. She taught him the alphabet and a few simple words. But when her husband found out, he ordered her to stop. Didn't she know it was against the law to teach a slave to read and write? He might get ideas about freedom. He might forge papers that said he was free. Then he could escape to a northern state where slavery was outlawed.

Frederick was determined to learn to read. He got lessons from poor white children he met on his errands. He paid for them with pieces of bread. As a teen, he read everything he could about the struggle against slavery. He resolved to escape. But how? Slaves who were caught escaping were killed or sold to slaveholders in the Deep South.

At age 20 Frederick saw his chance. His master had hired him out to a shipyard. He had learned the trade of repairing wooden ships. He had also met a free black woman named Anna Murray whom he was planning to marry. Frederick borrowed money from Anna. He got papers from a friend that certified him as free. Dressed as a sailor, he made his way by train and boat to New York City. He was free!

Frederick knew, however, that he could still be caught and sent back into slavery. He was afraid to look for a job or a place to live. Then he found a friend in David Ruggles, who worked for the Underground Railroad. This was a secret network of people helping slaves to escape. Ruggles hid Frederick in his home. He found him a job repairing ships in New Bedford, Massachusetts. There Frederick sent for Anna, and they were married. The couple stayed with Nathan Johnson, a wealthy black man. Johnson suggested that Frederick change his name to avoid capture. He chose the name of a character in a novel. Frederick Baily was now Frederick Douglass.

Under his new name, Frederick became famous. He wrote articles and gave lectures against slavery. He was a powerful speaker who described from his own experience the horrors of slavery. He carefully left out details that would identify him as the escaped slave Frederick Baily. But when people began to doubt his story, he decided to reveal all the facts. In 1845, he published his autobiography. It named people and places. It became a best-seller. But its author was safe from capture. He had sailed for England.

Frederick liked England. He knew his work lay in America, where his people were enslaved. But being captured was a real possibility. Then two English friends raised $710.96 to buy his freedom. They sent it to his legal "owner," Thomas Auld, who signed papers declaring him free. In the spring of 1847, Frederick Douglass came home.

1 How did Frederick learn to read?

A His master taught him.

B He read secretly at night.

C He went to a secret school.

D He paid children to teach him.

2 Tell about three elements of the escape plan Frederick used.

____

____

____

____

____

____

3 Explain how Frederick solved a problem by changing his name.

____

____

____

____

____

____

4 What problem did Frederick resolve by revealing his identity in his autobiography?

A He had to go to England to avoid capture.

B People doubted that his story was true.

C He needed money to continue his work.

D People wanted him to write about slavery.

5 What solution made it possible for him to return from England?

A Friends paid Thomas Auld for his freedom.

B The Civil War ended slavery in America.

C His autobiography had become a best-seller.

D He was much in demand as a speaker against slavery.

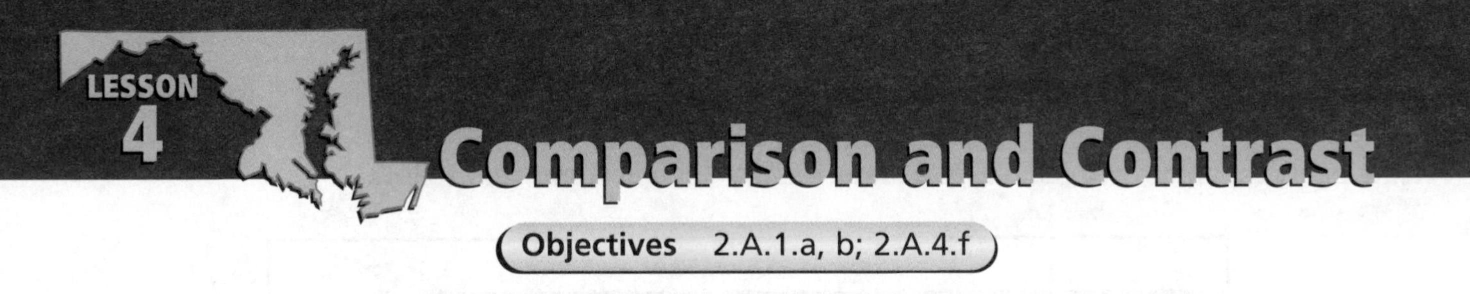

LESSON 4 Comparison and Contrast

Objectives 2.A.1.a, b; 2.A.4.f

Noticing similarities and differences as you read can help you organize information in your mind. When you note similarities between two things, actions, or ideas, you're comparing. When you note differences between them, you're contrasting.

This Venn diagram compares and contrasts two favorite animals:

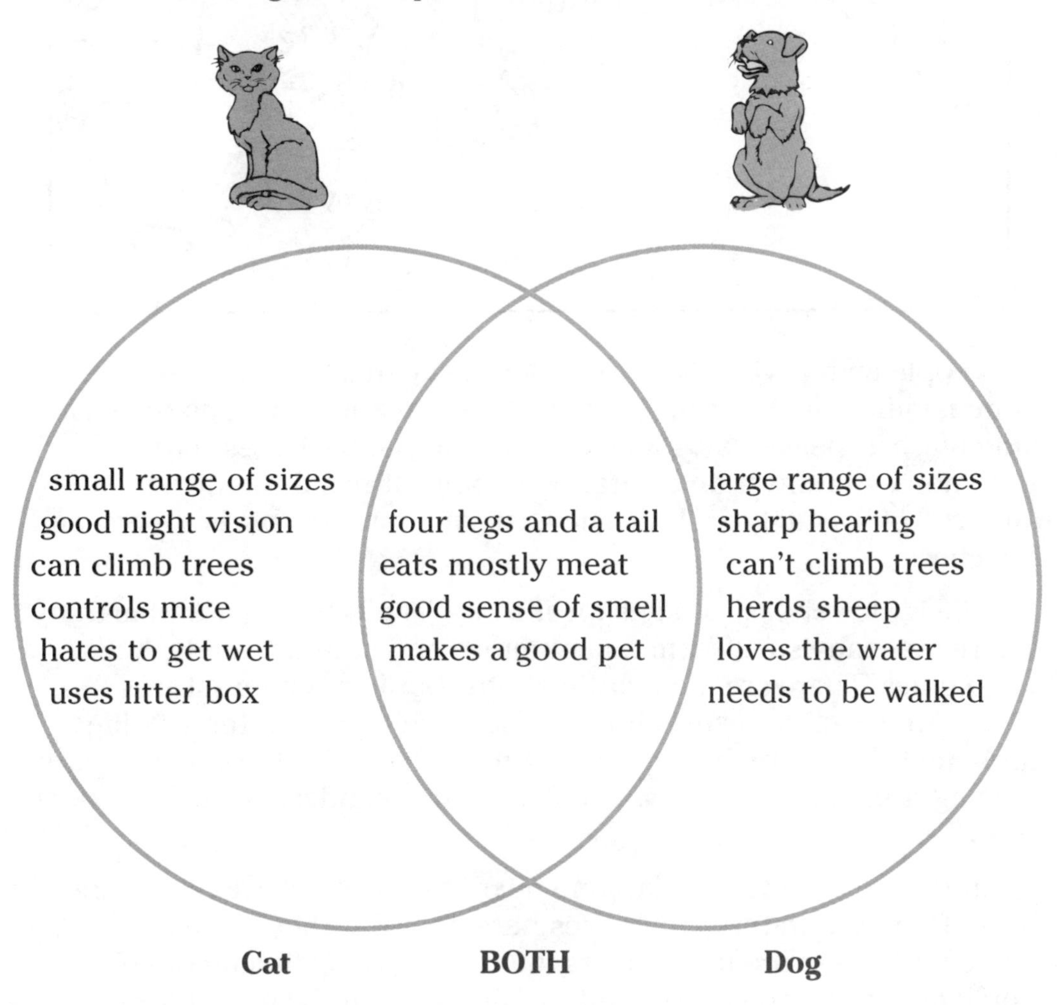

The middle of the diagram compares a cat and a dog. It shows how they are similar. The outer part of each circle shows how a cat and dog are different. They contrast the two animals.

Guided Practice

Read an article about two regions of a state. Answer the questions that follow.

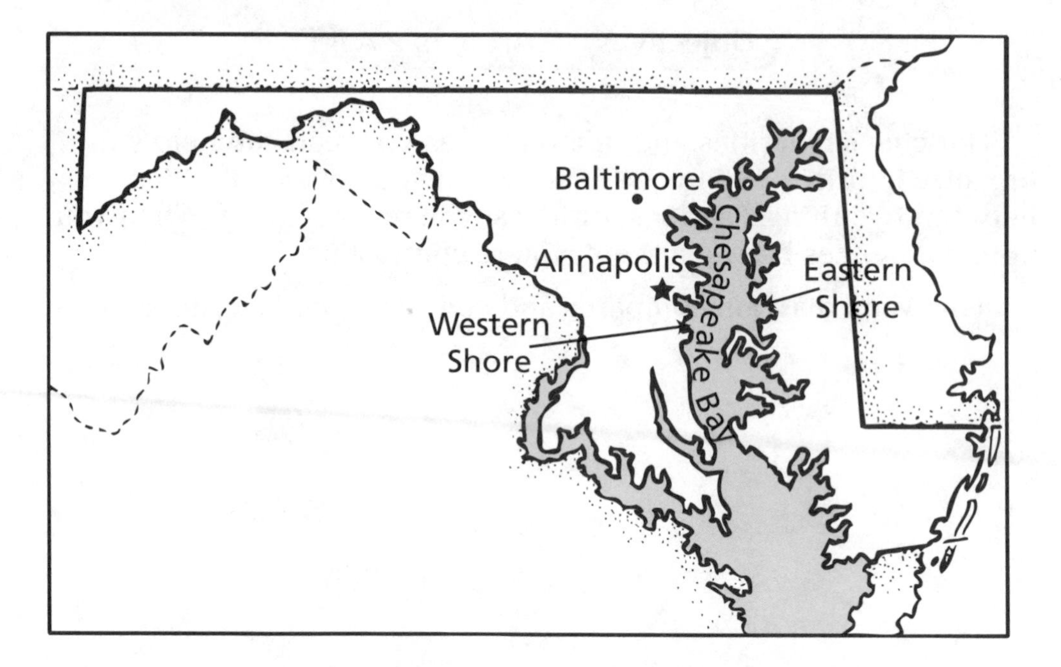

People on Maryland's Eastern Shore say that their part of the state is different. And they're right. "Eastern Shore" means the east side of Chesapeake Bay. The west has Maryland's largest city, Baltimore, and the state capital, Annapolis. It has the crowded suburbs of Washington, D.C. The Eastern Shore has birds, rivers, and beaches.

Life is slower east of Chesapeake Bay. The land is flat and marshy. There are many small farm communities and country roads, but no large cities. There are many little shops, but few "chain" stores. There are vacation resorts for visitors to enjoy the water, wildlife, and quiet. But there are also "waterman villages," where people earn a living from crabs, oysters, and fish as Marylanders have done since the 1600s.

In the Western Shore, flat land near the bay gives way to rolling hills. There are waterman villages here, too. But they are in museums. There are many boats, but few working fishing boats. You'll find mostly pleasure craft in Annapolis, and cargo ships in Baltimore's busy port. South of Baltimore, farmland is being covered by homes and shopping malls. Annapolis has the United States Naval Academy. The Navy also tests airplanes at a base on the Western Shore.

Of course neither shore of Chesapeake Bay is all one thing. The Western Shore has its share of vacation spots, old farmhouses, and peaceful rivers. Both regions boast state parks, great seafood, and historic sites. And you can get up-to-date health care or a video-game machine in many Eastern Shore communities as well as in Baltimore.

The author suggests that Maryland's Eastern Shore is "different" because it is ______.

- **A** old-fashioned
- **B** near the water
- **C** mostly built up
- **D** not crowded

The first paragraph contrasts the two regions. It describes the busy city life on the Western Shore. It says that what makes the Eastern Shore different are "birds, rivers, and beaches." So it's the west that's built up. Both sides are near the water. The last paragraph makes the point that the Eastern shore is not old-fashioned. It just has fewer people and a more relaxed way of life. So D is the correct answer.

According to the article, one thing you'll find on both the Eastern and Western shores is ______.

- **A** large cities
- **B** peaceful rivers
- **C** soaring mountains
- **D** fishing villages

The second paragraph describes the Eastern Shore's attractions. There are no large cities there. The third paragraph contrasts it with the Western Shore. Here, fishing villages are in museums. The Western Shore has "rolling hills," but there are no soaring mountains in either region. The last paragraph tells you that the Western Shore has peaceful rivers as well as does the Eastern. So B is the correct answer.

In what ways are both regions good places for a vacation? Tell about at least *two* ways.

____

____

____

____

____

____

Both regions are good for water sports and outdoor activities. Both have good seafood, historic sites, and state parks. The Western Shore has big-city attractions, while the Eastern Shore is more for people who want to be closer to nature.

On which shore would you be most likely to find "chain" stores?

A the Western Shore

B the Eastern Shore

C both

D neither

According to the article, the Eastern Shore has few "chain" stores. It also mentions shopping malls by contrast on the Western Shore. You know that "chain" stores are often found in shopping malls. So A is the correct answer

Now compare and contrast two advertisements and answer the questions that follow.

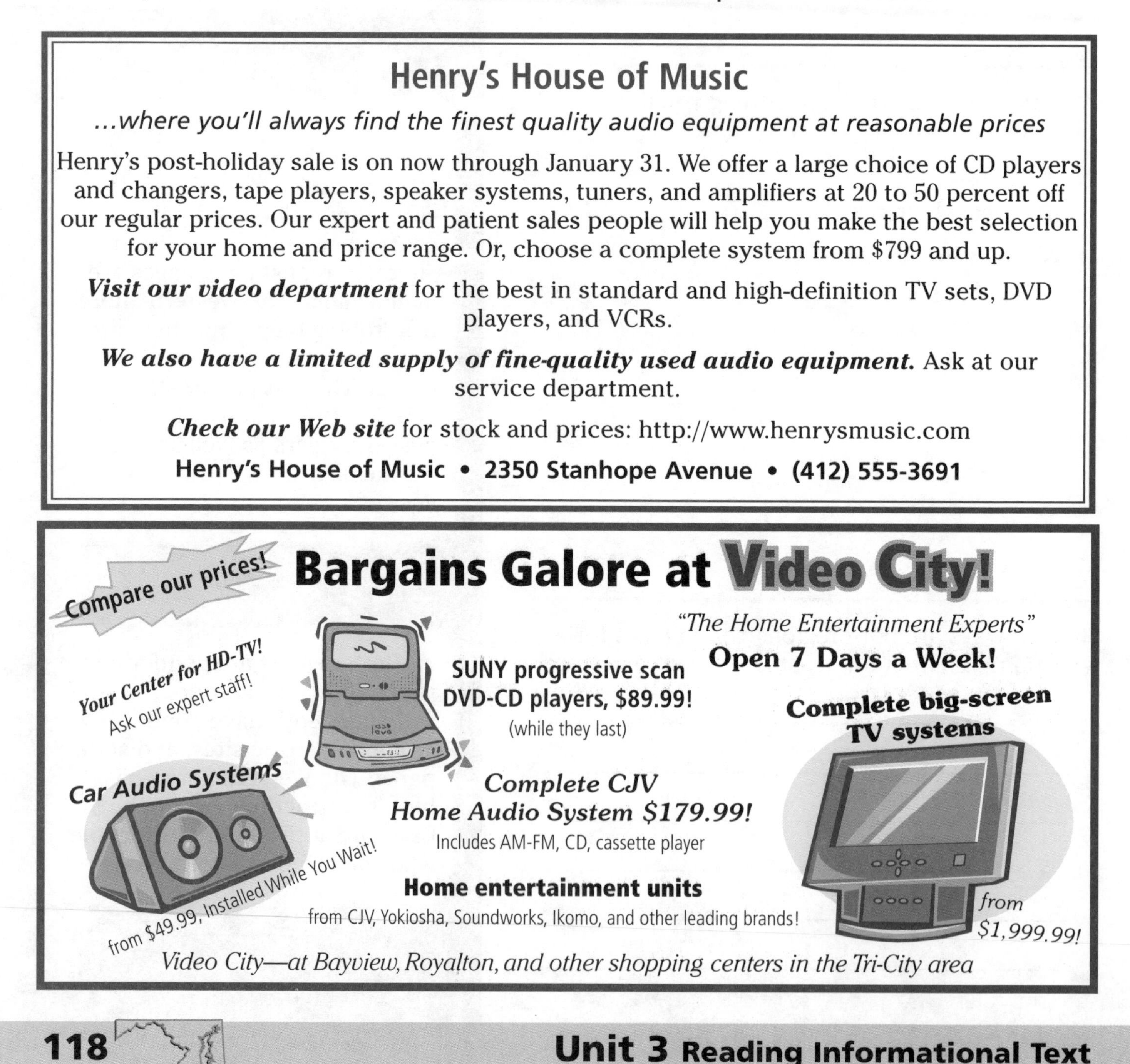

What is one thing that is the same about the two ads?

A They both advertise the "finest quality" goods.

B They both sell car audio systems.

C They both claim to be experts.

D They both list a Web site.

Only Henry's calls its stock "finest quality" and lists a Web site. Only Video City advertises car audio systems. Both stores claim, each in its own way, to be "experts." So C is the correct answer.

In which of these ways are the stores different?

A Henry's House of Music does not sell TV sets.

B You won't find any bargains at Henry's.

C You won't find anything over $1,000 at Video City

D One advertises specific brands, the other doesn't.

A look at the ads shows that Henry's does sell TV sets. Video City advertises one product at $1,999.99. Unlike Video City, Henry's doesn't advertise "Bargains Galore." But it is offering 20 to 50 percent off regular prices. Henry's ad, though, does not mention any brand names, while Video City's does. So D is the correct answer.

Which business has only one location?

A Henry's House of Music

B Video City

C both

D neither

A line at the bottom of each ad shows the stores' locations. Henry's House of Music has only one address, while Video City has several. The correct answer is A.

Both stores use features of print in their ads. What is one thing that is the *same* about how they use it? What is one thing that is *different?*

____

____

____

____

____

Both stores use large, bold type in headings. They use different fonts to print lines that they want you to notice. But Video City uses these features much more than Henry's House of Music. Almost every line of type has some eye-catching feature. Henry's also centers their type, while Video City places theirs in little blocks around the page.

Test Yourself

Read this selection about two sports. Answer the questions that follow.

My name is Anna DeWitt. I enjoy most sports, but I have two favorites. One is soccer. That's a game that's well known around the world. The other is lacrosse. That's a game not many people know. So let me tell you something about it.

You play lacrosse on a field that's about 60 yards wide and 110 yards long. That's about the same size as a soccer field. There's a ball too, as in soccer. In both games you score by shooting the ball into a goal with a net behind it. A score in both games is called a "goal." And in both games one player's job is to guard the goal.

That's about all that's similar between the two games. A soccer ball is a little smaller than a basketball. A lacrosse ball is about the size of a tennis ball. It's made of hard rubber. If you get smacked with it, you feel it. And believe me, you get smacked.

In soccer, you move the ball mostly by kicking it. In lacrosse, you use a long stick with a little net basket on one end. You catch the ball in the basket. You can run with it, pass it to a teammate, or try to throw it into the goal. You also can hit your opponents' sticks with yours to try to knock the ball loose. It's a foul and a penalty if you hit *them*. As in soccer, only the goalkeeper may touch the ball with her hands.

In soccer, the rules for men and women are the same. In lacrosse, there are differences. For one, some players on a men's team use a stick up to 72 inches long. The limit for women is 44 inches. There are 10 players on a men's lacrosse team, but 12 on a women's team. A men's lacrosse game is divided into four 15-minute quarters. Women play two 30-minute halves. Men are allowed to bump each other. Women aren't. I don't know whether or not that's fair, but those are the rules.

In soccer, of course, there are eleven players on a side and a game is 90 minutes no matter who's playing. There is more scoring in lacrosse too, even though the goal is much smaller. A good game might end up 15-13. A soccer team that gives up 13 goals is in trouble!

Soccer was invented in England and spread all over the world. Lacrosse is about as American as you can get. It was invented by Native Americans, who called it "the little brother of war." It's especially popular in Canada, but it's also played in the United States and Europe. I'd love to see it become as big as soccer!

1 How are soccer and lacrosse alike?

A The fields are about the same size.

B The balls are about the same size.

C You move the balls mostly by kicking them.

D Both games are well known around the world.

2 One way soccer and lacrosse are different is that ______.

A in soccer, only the goalkeeper may touch the ball with the hands

B in lacrosse, you shoot a ball into a goal with a net behind it

C in soccer, there are 11 players on a side

D in lacrosse, you can pass the ball to a teammate

3 "The game was invented by Native Americans." This statement refers to ______.

A soccer

B lacrosse

C both games

D neither game

4 What is the same about scoring in lacrosse and in soccer? What is different? Identify *two* similarities and *two* differences.

____

____

____

____

____

____

5 In both soccer and lacrosse ______.

A there are 11 players on a side

B the game is 90 minutes long

C you catch and pass the ball with a stick

D one player's job is to guard the goal

6 "The stick may be up to 72 inches long." That rule applies to lacrosse as played by ______.

A men

B women

C both men and women

D nobody

7 Compare and contrast the rules of lacrosse for men and for women. Identify *three* ways they are the same and *three* ways they are different.

____

____

____

____

____

____

Author's Purpose and Audience

Objectives 2.A.1.a, b; 2.A.4.a, b; 2.A.6.d

Authors have many different reasons, or purposes, for writing. When you read for information, ask yourself *why* the author is writing, *who* the audience is, and *how* the information is being presented.

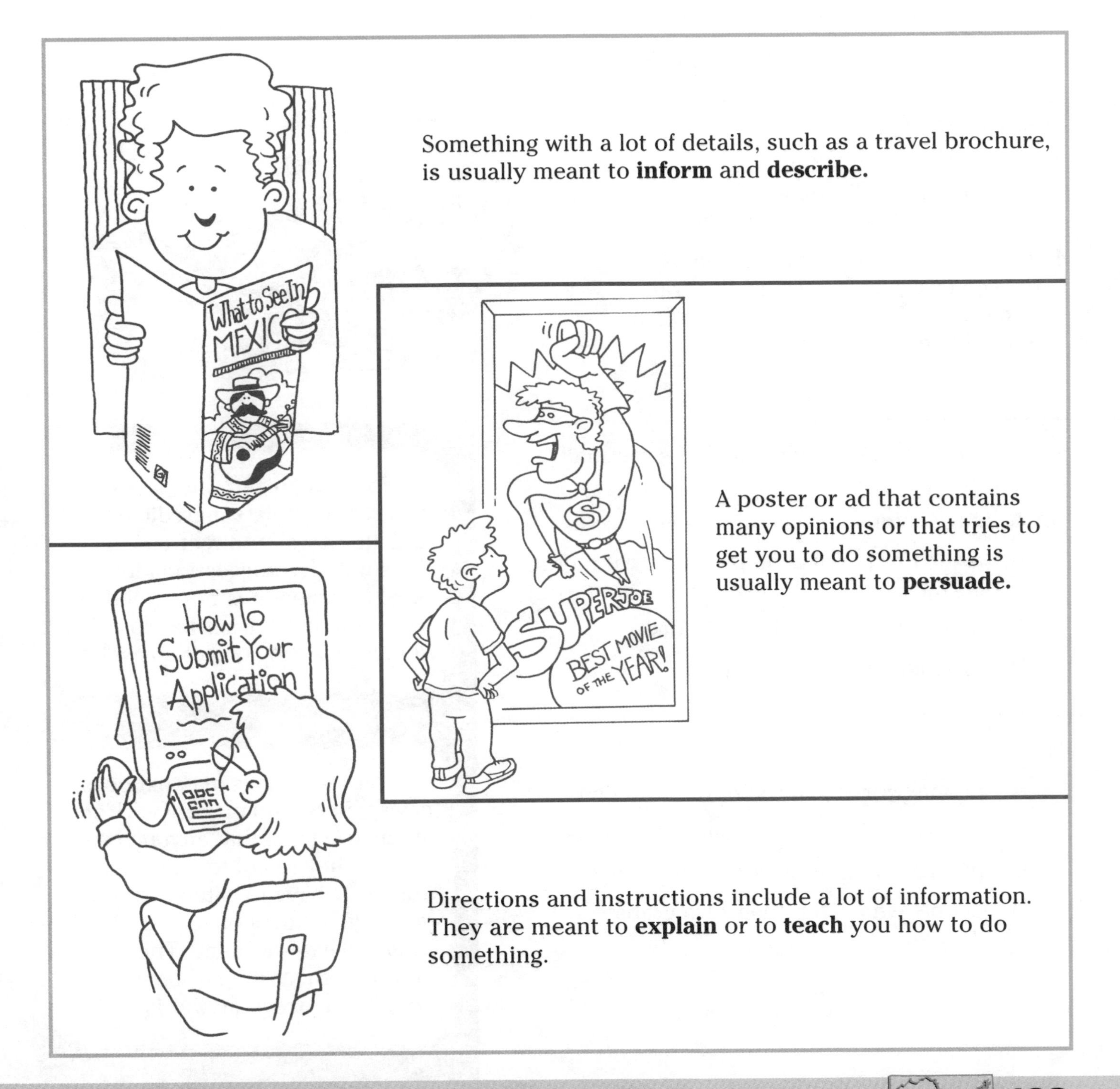

Something with a lot of details, such as a travel brochure, is usually meant to **inform** and **describe.**

A poster or ad that contains many opinions or that tries to get you to do something is usually meant to **persuade.**

Directions and instructions include a lot of information. They are meant to **explain** or to **teach** you how to do something.

Guided Practice

Read this passage and answer the questions that follow.

Maryland Crab Cakes

1 pound crab meat
1 cup bread or cracker crumbs
1 large egg, beaten
$\frac{1}{4}$ cup mayonnaise
$\frac{1}{2}$ teaspoon salt
$\frac{1}{4}$ teaspoon pepper
1 teaspoon Worcestershire sauce
1 teaspoon dry mustard
oil for frying

1. Pick over crabmeat to remove gristle.
2. In a large bowl, mix crumbs, eggs, mayonnaise, and seasonings.
3. Add crab meat. Mix gently but thoroughly. If too dry, add a little more mayonnaise. Shape into six cakes.
4. In a heavy pan, heat just enough oil to keep cakes from sticking. Fry crab cakes about 5 minutes on each side or until brown.

Which choice *best* tells what kind of selection this is?

- **A** suggestions for planning a meal
- **B** an article persuading people to eat more seafood
- **C** a description of a delicious dish
- **D** instructions for cooking

You recognized this passage as a recipe. It lists ingredients and step-by step directions. It does not give suggestions for meal planning. It is not intended to persuade or describe. So choice D is the correct answer.

The author is writing for ______.

- **A** people working in their home kitchens
- **B** expert cooks in restaurants and hotels
- **C** people trying to decide where to eat
- **D** people who catch their own crabs

You see recipes in cookbooks, newspapers, and magazines. They are instructions that anyone can follow. They're not for experts. You don't have to catch the crabs yourself. Readers have decided *where* to eat—at home. The author is suggesting *what* and *how*. The correct answer is A.

Tell about *three* things the author does to help achieve his purpose.

____

____

____

____

____

The recipe lists all ingredients to help cooks plan. Instructions are numbered so that readers can follow them easily. When bowls or pans are called for, the author tells you so at the beginning of the instruction.

Now read this selection and answer the questions that follow.

Dear Karin,

I haven't unpacked my computer yet, so I'm sending this to you the old-fashioned way. I already miss you and the neighborhood, but this will be a wonderful place to spend the summer. The house is really old. It has three stories. All the windows on the upper floors have little peaks over them. There's an attic and all kinds of odd closets that will be fun to explore. The best thing about it is the back yard. It's huge, with a shady oak tree in the middle and hedges all around. Mom says we'll need to buy some goats to keep the grass trimmed. I don't think she's serious. I'll send you some pictures soon.

Love,

Dorinda

What *best* describes the main purpose of this selection?

A to persuade Karin to come to visit

B to record Dorinda's private thoughts and feelings

C to describe the house and its back yard

D to teach readers about an old style of home building

You probably recognized the passage as a friendly letter. The purpose of a friendly letter is usually to share thoughts and feelings with others. To record private thoughts and feelings, Dorinda would use a diary. The letter doesn't include facts about home building. The only details are about what the house and yard look like and how Dorinda feels about them. She mentions that she misses Karin, but she doesn't try to persuade her to visit. The correct answer is C.

You knew that your answer to the first question is correct because the selection *mainly* ______.

A contains details about what things look like

B includes a joking comment about goats

C gives a lot of facts and detailed instructions

D is about how much Dorinda misses Karin

Dorinda's letter contains many details about what things look like, choice A. Although she might write to give facts, be funny, or tell her friend she misses her, in a friendly letter, people usually describe what they do and see.

Now read part of a pamphlet and answer the questions that follow.

Biking the C & O

Ride through history along the famous Chesapeake and Ohio Canal. The "C & O" runs 184.5 miles from Cumberland, Maryland, to Washington, D.C. Follow the route of canal boats of 150 years ago, managed and preserved by the National Park Service. Big trees shading the old towpath make it a comfortable ride.

Join the thousands of bicyclists, hikers, and horseback riders who enjoy the canal every year. Ride the entire route and stop at campgrounds or inns along the way. Or, just make it an easy one-day trip along part of the canal. You may have trouble deciding which part, though, as the route offers many attractions. There's the beautiful scenery of the Maryland mountains and the Great Falls of the Potomac River. There are the historic Civil War battlefields of Antietam and Balls Bluff. Wildlife lovers keep an eye out for deer, small mammals, and birds, including Maryland's famous Great Blue Herons.

Bike shops in towns along the route provide service, spare parts, and friendly assistance. For further information contact the C&O National Historic Park, P.O. Box 4, Sharpsburg, MD 21782 or on the World Wide Web at http://www.nps.gov/choh/

The author's *main* purpose in writing this selection is to ______.

- **A** persuade visitors to ride bikes instead of driving
- **B** persuade bicyclists to ride the C&O Canal route
- **C** inform readers about the C&O Canal's interesting history
- **D** describe scenery and wildlife along the canal route

The selection does include information about history and scenery. But this information only supports the author's purpose: making biking the route appeal to readers. Words like *famous, comfortable, enjoy, easy, beautiful,* and *friendly* suggest that the selection is meant to persuade. But there is no mention of cars. The correct answer is B.

The author's intended audience is *mostly* ______.

- **A** world-class mountain bikers
- **B** children who ride bikes to school
- **C** adults and families with bicycles
- **D** hikers, horseback riders, and bicyclists

Words like "easy" and "comfortable" probably wouldn't persuade world-class mountain bikers. Children would not be deciding to ride a trail in a national park without adults. The passage mentions that the path is used by hikers and horseback riders. Its appeal, however, is aimed at bicycle riders. The correct answer is C.

What does the author do in this selection to achieve her purpose? Name at least *three* things.

____

____

____

____

____

____

The author makes it sound like an adventure by mentioning the length of the ride (184.5 miles) and the history of the canal's use. But she also makes sure it doesn't sound too difficult by mentioning stops and services along the way and by suggesting that people may only ride part of the trail. Descriptions of the trail will appeal to people who like scenery, history, or wildlife. The address and Web site make it easy for people to get more information.

Test Yourself

Now read three more selections about the Chesapeake and Ohio Canal. Answer the questions that follow the third selection.

Selection 1

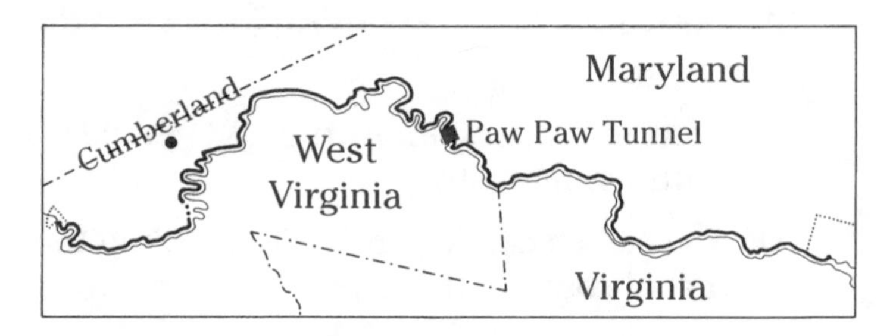

The canal was proposed by none other than George Washington. He owned land in the western part of Virginia. He thought a canal would attract settlers. It could bring city goods to their farms and carry their farm produce to markets in the east. But it wasn't until 1828, long after Washington was dead, that work on the canal began.

The canal was six feet deep and 40 to 60 feet wide. It included 74 locks, seven dams, and a 3,118–foot tunnel near Oldtown, Maryland. It was called the Chesapeake and Ohio Canal because it was meant to reach all the way to the Ohio River. But construction was slow. When it reached Cumberland, Maryland, in 1850, it stopped altogether.

The reason it stopped was one that George Washington could never have dreamed of—railroads. Construction of the Baltimore and Ohio Railroad began on the same day construction began on the canal. By 1870, canal boats were moving almost a million tons of freight a year. But the railroad carried more and moved it faster. Two big floods, in 1889 and 1924, put the canal out of business. Today, the canal and its towpath are preserved in a national park.

Selection 2

The Paw Paw Inn

Enjoy country comfort with modern conveniences at our gracious bed-and-breakfast inn. Our 150-year-old farmhouse offers six unique guest bedrooms. All rooms feature pictures and artifacts from 250 years of our region's history. Full breakfast is served in our dining room every day from May through October.

We're located in Paw Paw, Maryland, off state route 51, with easy access to antique shopping, biking, the Chesapeake and Ohio Canal National Historic Park, and Green Ridge State Forest. Children 12 or older are welcome.

For reservations contact Jim & Janis, (301) 555-6375, or http://www.pawpawinn.com

Selection 3

The Paw Paw Tunnel on the Chesapeake and Ohio Canal is located near Mile 156. **It is illegal to ride bicycles in the tunnel.** If you're on a bike, you'll need to get off and walk. You'll need to carry a flashlight, too. Except for a pinpoint of light at either end, there is total darkness for most of the tunnel's 0.6-mile length.

The trail inside the tunnel is straight and mostly dry. Train your flashlight on the ceiling here and there. The white brick reflects the light in interesting ways. Near the upstream (western) end, the trail is muddier. You may be splashed by water dripping from the ceiling.

Scenery is spectacular at either end of the tunnel. The cliffs and waterfalls on the western side are especially breathtaking. In summer, you may see turtles sunning themselves on logs.

1 The author's purpose in Selection 1 is to ______.

A explain something of the history of the canal

B relate a little-known fact about George Washington

C describe the historic places along the canal route

D persuade people to visit the national park

2 Which of these is a clue in Selection 1 that suggests the author's purpose?

A details about points of interest

B details about how the canal was built

C the use of addresses and phone numbers

D the use of dates and figures

3 The author's purpose in Selection 2 is to ______.

A describe the rooms at the Paw Paw Inn

B get visitors to stay at the Paw Paw Inn

C bring shoppers to nearby stores

D relate the history of a 150-year-old house

4 What does the author of Selection 2 do to achieve this purpose? Give at least *three* examples.

____

____

____

____

____

____

5 The author's purpose in Selection 3 is to ______.

A warn people of the dangers of the Paw Paw Tunnel

B tell the story of how the Paw Paw Tunnel was built

C encourage bicycle riders to use the Paw Paw Tunnel

D describe the Paw Paw Tunnel and its surroundings

6 How does the tone of Selections 2 and 3 show you that they are meant for different audiences? Give at least *two* examples from each selection.

____

____

____

____

____

____

7 Which of these selections would you be *most likely* to find in a traveler's personal account of the Chesapeake and Ohio Canal?

A Selection 1

B Selection 2

C Selection 3

D All are equally likely.

Fact and Opinion

Objectives 2.A.1.a, b; 2.A.4.b, h; 2.A.6.d

When you read nonfiction, you are reading facts—mostly. Some of the statements you read may be the author's opinions. As you read you need to distinguish the author's opinions from facts. A fact is a statement that can be proved. An opinion tells you how someone thinks and feels about something. It is a statement that the author can't possibly know is a fact.

These words can be clues that the author is expressing an opinion:

Guided Practice

Read a student's letter to a school principal. Answer the questions that follow.

Dear Ms. Kleyn,

Winter has arrived. Snow is all over the school playground. It should be a time for fun. But no one is happy at recess. Why? Snowball fights are not allowed.

This is the first letter I ever sent to you. But I feel that this rule should be changed. No one really gets hurt in a snowball fight. And everyone thinks they're fun. Please, Ms. Kleyn, change the rule.

In which of these sentences does the author give an opinion?

- **A** Winter has arrived.
- **B** Snow is all over the school playground.
- **C** But no one is happy at recess.
- **D** Snowball fights are not allowed.

The writer of the letter could easily prove that it was winter and that snow is on the ground (choices A and B). The writer would not be writing the letter if there wasn't a school rule against snowball fights (choice D). But the author could not prove that "no one is happy" at recess (choice C). Some students may be happy. The correct answer is choice C. It expresses a belief that the author has not proved.

Which of these sentences states a fact?

- **A** This is the first letter I ever sent to you.
- **B** But I feel that this rule should be changed.
- **C** No one really gets hurt in a snowball fight.
- **D** And everyone thinks they're fun.

Here a number of words give you clues to which of the choices are opinions. Words like *I feel, everyone* and *should* point to opinions. Choice B cannot be right, since it is only what the author feels. You know that choice C cannot be a fact. People do get hurt in snowball fights. Maybe there are some people who think snowball fights are not fun. So choice D is not correct. Choice A is a fact. The letter writer or the principal could prove it. So choice A is correct.

In the first paragraph, does the sentence "It should be a time for fun" state a fact or the author's opinion? Explain why.

____

____

____

____

____

The word *should* gives you a clue. It's a feeling word. Who says winter "should" be a time for fun? The author does. But what about the author's mom, for instance, who may have to drive to work through snow and ice? The sentence is the author's opinion.

Now read this book report. Answer the questions that follow.

Conqueror's March by Aníbal Solís

Conqueror's March is about Spanish explorers in America. I found it an exciting adventure story that keeps you reading. The book is about a true event that happened in the 1500s. The author tells the story like a novel, but his characters are real people.

The hero is Alvar Nuñez Cabeza de Vaca. He was a brave soldier of the king of Spain. In 1527, he was second-in-command of an expedition to Florida. The leader, Narváez, was greedy, foolish, and crazy. He did not know the country, and he was interested only in gold. Because of his mistakes, Narváez's men got lost and ran out of food. Then he was killed in a storm at sea. Cabeza de Vaca had to lead the survivors to safety in Mexico.

He did this after a number of amazing adventures. He and the others were captured by Indians near what is now Houston, Texas. They were made slaves. Only four men were still alive when they escaped six years later. They made their way across plains, rivers, and deserts. Finally, in 1536, they reached Mexico City.

I think *Conqueror's March* is a really good book. Everyone interested in history will like it. The title really is the opposite of what the book describes. The Spanish did conquer much of America. They made slaves of the Indians. Cabeza de Vaca and his men thought they would be conquerors. They came to America for land and gold. But they themselves became slaves and ended up running for their lives. Even if you don't care about these things, *Conqueror's March* is still an exciting story.

Which of these sentences is *not* a fact?

A It is an exciting adventure story that keeps you reading.

B *Conqueror's March* is about Spanish explorers in America.

C The book is about a true event that happened in the 1500s.

D The author tells the story like a novel, but his characters are real people.

The correct answer is A. All the other choices are statements that can be proved. You cannot prove that the book is "exciting." That is the opinion of the author of the book report. Maybe if you read the book, you would not think it is exciting.

Which of these sentences is an opinion?

- **A** Alvar Nuñez Cabeza de Vaca was a soldier of the king of Spain.
- **B** In 1527, he was second-in-command of an expedition to Florida.
- **C** The leader, Narváez, was greedy, foolish, and crazy.
- **D** Narváez's men got lost and ran out of food.

C is the correct answer. This is the only choice that cannot be proved. You could prove choices A and B by looking them up in a history book. There is probably evidence for choice D, too.

The author is giving an opinion by saying ______.

- **A** He did this after a number of amazing adventures.
- **B** Then he was killed in a storm at sea.
- **C** Four men were still alive when they escaped six years later.
- **D** Finally, in 1536, they reached Mexico City.

You can't prove that Cabeza de Vaca's adventures were "amazing." They may amaze *some* people. But you cannot take it as a fact. So choice A is correct. All the other choices are facts. Most likely, people who were alive in 1536 wrote down what happened.

Which of these sentences from the passage states a fact?

- **A** I think *Conqueror's March* is a really good book.
- **B** Everyone interested in history will like it.
- **C** The Spanish did conquer much of America.
- **D** He was a brave soldier of the king of Spain.

Only one statement here can be proved. That is choice C. You could look it up. The other statements are opinions. Someone else might not think *Conqueror's March* is a "really good book." Some people interested in history might not like it. Some people might not think Cabeza de Vaca was "brave." Statements about what people think are really what the report's author thinks. Choice C is correct.

Can you prove this statement to be true: "They came to America for land and gold"? Explain why or why not.

____

____

____

____

____

____

A book about history might tell you that early Spanish explorers in America were indeed looking for land and gold. But was that true of all of them? Specifically, was it true of Cabeza de Vaca and his men? These were individual people who had their own individual reasons for venturing into unknown land. The author of the book report could not know these reasons. The statement is the author's opinion.

Test Yourself

Now read an article about another figure from history. Answer the questions that follow.

Ishi

Ishi came down from the mountains in August, 1911. That's when his sad and fascinating story begins. Ishi was not his real name. By tradition, the Yahi people did not reveal their names. Ishi means "man" in the Yahi language. He was the last living speaker of that language.

Everyone knows what happened to America's native peoples when European settlers moved in. It is a shameful tale of murder and terror. The Yana and Yahi were related tribes in northern California. Early in the 1800s, they numbered about 20,000. By 1870, there were only about 400 left. The rest had become sick or had been killed. Ishi was one of a small Yahi band. They lived secretly in the woods near the town of Oroville. One by one they died, until only Ishi was left. Desperate and hungry, he stumbled into town, perhaps hoping he would find a warm welcome there. Instead, he was held in jail until Thomas Waterman rescued him.

Waterman was a scientist at the University of California. He studied different people and cultures. Waterman took Ishi to the university's museum in San Francisco. The museum director was Alfred Kroeber, another scientist. Kroeber took a liking to their friendly and smart guest. He invited Ishi to live at the museum.

Today, people would say that Kroeber "used" Ishi. But Kroeber saw himself as Ishi's protector and friend. He advertised Ishi as "the last stone-age Indian in North America." He had Ishi demonstrate his people's traditional crafts to museum visitors. Ishi showed them how he built fires and made arrows. He worked with a scholar to record his people's language.

Kroeber was in Europe in 1916 when he got the news that Ishi had died. He sent a letter back to the university. He ordered that no study should be made of Ishi's body. But the letter arrived too late. A study was made of Ishi's body. Then, he was buried in San Francisco.

Ishi's story does not end there. People today believe that the bodies of Indians belong to their people, not to museums. In 1997, Native Americans in California started a movement to bring Ishi home. His body was dug up from a San Francisco cemetery. Then it was buried in the Yahi homeland. Ishi, last of his people, at last returned home to rest among them.

1 Which of these sentences does *not* state a fact?

- **A** Ishi came down from the mountains in August, 1911.
- **B** That is where his sad and fascinating story begins.
- **C** By tradition, the Yahi people did not reveal their names.
- **D** Ishi was the last living speaker of the Yahi language.

2 Which of these sentences from the article is a fact?

- **A** Everyone knows what happened to America's native peoples when European settlers arrived.
- **B** It is a shameful story of murder and terror.
- **C** The Yana and Yahi were related tribes in northern California.
- **D** Cold and hungry, he stumbled into town, perhaps hoping he would find a warm welcome there.

3 Based on the article, which of the following statements is a fact?

- **A** Ishi was friendly and smart.
- **B** For a time, Ishi lived in a museum.
- **C** Kroeber "used" Ishi as an exhibit.
- **D** Ishi's body should not have been buried.

4 Which of the following is an opinion?

A In 1997, Native Americans led a movement to have Ishi buried in his homeland.

B At the museum, Ishi worked with someone to help write down his language.

C The bodies of Indians belong to their people.

D After Ishi first entered the town, he was put in jail.

5 Explain whether this statement is or is *not* an opinion of the author: "Ishi showed museum visitors how to make arrows."

____

____

____

____

____

____

LESSON 7

Analyzing Language in Informational Text

Objectives 2.A.1.a, b; 2.A.5.a, b; 2.A.6.f

Words don't always mean what they say. For instance, if you're annoyed at your little brother who keeps throwing a ball at you, you might say "Cut it out!" He may know the meaning of each of these words individually. But unless he knows that *cut it out* means "stop it," he's going to keep bothering you.

When you read, you often have to **analyze language.** Someone is trying to get a message to you. But the message isn't always contained in the exact meaning of words.

Guided Practice

Read a movie review. Then answer the questions that follow.

The summer's funniest movie opened this week. *New Kid on the Planet* is the story of Joshua Mbele. Joshua and his family are going to spend two years on Styonar. That's the planet where the flying saucers come from. Joshua's parents are experts on the aliens and their world. His father translates Styonari books into English. His mother studies Styonari science. But to Joshua, the two years loom like a life sentence. The aliens and everything about them make him squirm.

Jamaal Philips is outstanding as Joshua. He's every kid in a new school, worried about whether the kids will think he's cool and whether he might say something that will get him beaten up. This familiar story is blown out of shape by the fact that the other kids are flying reptiles. You can feel how nervous Joshua is among them. But his parents want him to fit in, so they send him off for a day with some alien kids. That's when the story takes off. You'll laugh when a curious crowd surrounds Joshua at a shopping mall. You'll be grossed out when he discovers what he's eating at a snack bar. The funniest part comes when Joshua tries to teach his new friends how to play football.

Of course he *does* make friends. You can spot the ending a mile away, but that's OK. Summer Blades is fine as Joshua's wise mother. Charles Mills is funny as his dad. He's a walking encyclopedia on Styonari culture and loves everything about them to the point of ridiculousness. The aliens are computer-graphics creations. They're so realistic they'll make your jaw drop, and so will the sets. *I'd* want to spend two years on Styonar, and so would you. But we'll have to settle for a couple of fun hours at the movies.

The review says that for Joshua, two years on Styonar "loom like a life sentence." This means that Joshua ______.

- **A** thinks he'll die in space
- **B** feels like he's going to prison
- **C** thinks it's going to be boring
- **D** is worried that he might actually like it

Like a life sentence is an example of figurative language. It helps you picture what Joshua is feeling. In his mind, Joshua is comparing two years on Styonar to something else. He's not comparing it to dying, and he certainly isn't expecting to like it. Boredom is not what he's worried about either. "Life sentence" refers to a term in prison—and that's what Joshua thinks Styonar will be like. The answer is B.

The reviewer says that the story "takes off" when Joshua goes off with the alien kids. What does "takes off" mean here?

- **A** starts to fly
- **B** turns strange
- **C** copies other stories
- **D** gets started

Takes off is another example of figurative language. It doesn't have anything to do with the usual meanings of *takes* or *off.* The phrase can refer to an airplane, but that's plainly not what it means here. Which of the choices can mean action *like* an airplane—getting going in a hurry? The movie has introduced the characters and the conflict. Now Joshua has to deal with the conflict. The only answer that makes sense is D.

What are some other examples in this passage of words that help you picture or feel something, or that have a meaning different from their usual meaning? Show at least *three* and explain what they mean.

____

____

____

____

____

Blown out of shape means "put into a funny and unfamiliar form." *Grossed out* means "disgusted." *A walking encyclopedia* compares the character of Joshua's dad to a reference book, crammed with facts. That's three. Can you find three others?

The reviewer uses the word "you" a great deal. This is meant to ______.

- **A** make readers agree with the reviewer
- **B** sound like a TV news announcer
- **C** imitate the feeling of watching the movie
- **D** establish a friendly, personal tone

Words can be used to create tone. Using the word "you" won't make readers agree or disagree unless they have seen the movie. But the use of "you" can make readers feel as if the reviewer were speaking personally to them. So D is the correct answer.

Now read a poster advertising the same movie. Answer the questions that follow.

What phrase on the poster means "big success"?

A smash hit

B like you're among aliens

C falling-down funny

D no passes accepted

Here you're being asked to recognize figurative language. Decide which choice makes sense as a way of saying "big success." Being compared to living among aliens does not suggest success, nor does falling down with laughter. "No passes accepted" may be a sign that a movie is a success, but it doesn't *mean* big success. "Smash hit" does. So the correct answer is A.

The phrase "rolling in the aisles" means ______.

A making a disturbance in the theater

B laughing so hard that you lose control

C making a lot of money

D losing your step in the dark

A clue here is that the phrase describes the word *funny*. Nobody really laughs so hard that they fall down and roll in the aisles. It's an exaggeration that makes a point about the movie. Try the other choices to see if they make sense. You'll see that the correct answer is B.

The person who designed the poster uses several effects of language to create tone. Which of these does the designer *not* use?

A repeated descriptive words

B repeated exclamation points

C serious, thoughtful expressions

D short, catchy phrases

The designer wants people to know that this movie is fun. The word funny is taken out of several reviews and used for effect. Every descriptive line is short, catchy, and ends with an exclamation point. Serious, thoughtful expressions would be out of place in a poster advertising a movie like this. The correct answer is C.

Some people who enjoy movies about outer space don't care for comedies. The opposite is true as well. How does the poster speak to people who like *both* types of movies?

____

____

____

____

____

The poster appeals to science-fiction fans with the word "planet" in the title and the word "aliens" in the description of the film. The illustration makes it clear that the move does not take place on Earth. The poster also makes it clear that the movie is a comedy by repeating the word *funny* in capitals several times.

Test Yourself

Read the following article about a private vacation spot and answer the questions that follow.

The forest is dark, damp, and deep. The only sounds are the rustle of leaves and the drip and plop of water. Just 70 miles from here, the swarming hive that is Washington, D.C. simmers in the July sun. But here in Catoctin Mountain Park, all is cool, quiet, and calm.

President Carter hosts the Camp David Peace Accords.

And yet...why is there a security fence here? What could be behind it? Why are United States Marines standing watch in a state park? Now the whap-whap of a helicopter breaks the silence. It grows louder, powering in from the southeast. It circles the fenced-in compound and settles in for a landing. More Marines surround the chopper as its engines power down. They salute as a familiar figure emerges—their Commander-in-Chief. "Welcome back to Camp David, Mr. President," says a Marine.

Camp David, Maryland, has been a place for our presidents to get away from it all since 1942. That was when President Franklin D. Roosevelt first used it as a comfortable nearby retreat from the capital's muggy summer climate. Roosevelt called it Shangri-La, after a hidden mountain city in a popular novel. It was President Dwight D. Eisenhower in 1953 who renamed it Camp David, after his grandson.

Camp David is a place where the president can relax and unwind. It has practice areas for golf, a gym, tennis courts, and a swimming pool. It has many comfortable guest cabins. President Harry Truman liked to take walks in the woods there. President Gerald Ford rode a snowmobile around the grounds. President Ronald Reagan preferred a horse. President George H.W. Bush celebrated his daughter's wedding there. But while Camp David is a place where presidents can take it easy, it is also where they host important foreign visitors. From these private meetings, earth-shaking events may result.

At Camp David, President Roosevelt and British leader Winston Churchill planned the strategy that would win World War II.

At Camp David, President Eisenhower and Soviet leader Nikita Khrushchev held talks that preserved peace between their two nations.

At Camp David, President Jimmy Carter hosted the leaders of two countries at war and helped them hammer out a peace agreement.

In the park that encircles Camp David, ordinary Americans enjoy camping, fishing, hiking, and picnicking. Meanwhile, just beyond the trees, history might be in the making.

1 In the second sentence, the words *plop* and *rustle* sound like what they mean. Which of these phrases from the passage also contains a word that sounds like what it means?

A cool, quiet, and calm

B muggy summer climate

C whap-whap of a helicopter

D earth-shaking events

2 "The swarming hive that is Washington, D.C. simmers in the July sun." The author here is trying to show that Washington is ______.

A noisy and exciting

B dark and dangerous

C fast and powerful

D busy and hot

3 What are some ways that the author creates a tone of mystery in the first two paragraphs? Give at least *three* examples and explain how each contributes to this tone.

____

____

____

____

____

____

4 "Take it easy" and "unwind" both are expressions that mean "relax." What other phrase in the article means the same thing?

A powering in

B get away from it all

C hidden mountain city

D take walks in the woods

5 In the second paragraph, "standing watch" is an expression that means ______.

A noting the time

B admiring the view

C marching and drilling

D on guard duty

6 To get a message across, the author uses several writing techniques. Which of these techniques is *not* used by the author?

A contrasting two different feelings

B repeating a short phrase several times

C using punctuation to gain attention

D taking a serious tone about events

7 President Carter helped "hammer out a peace agreement" between two warring nations. Explain what this phrase means and what the author is comparing the process to.

____

____

____

____

____

____

Unit 4: Reading Literary Text

What does "literary" mean? It means the reading you do for enjoyment. Literary selections include narratives, plays, and poems. In this unit you will learn about all three.

To talk about literary text—and to answer test questions—you need to know some special vocabulary. In this unit you will learn the important terms that people use to talk about literature.

There are four lessons in this unit:

1 **Elements of a Narrative** The narrative literary selections you read at school are usually fiction. The characters are not real people, and the story is made up. Fiction includes stories and novels. You probably read realistic fiction most often. Those are stories that are like real life. Historical fiction is also realistic. Since it is about a specific time in history, it includes interesting historical details.

You also read fables, fairy tales, and folktales. Mostly they are stories with a lesson or moral. You may also enjoy fantasy stories, such as the Harry Potter books or the Chronicles of Narnia. All of these kinds of books and stories are narratives.

2 **Plays and Poetry** Plays and poetry have very specific structures. You need to be able to recognize them and understand how they make the play or poem work.

3 **Analyzing Character** The characters are the most important part of a story. This lesson will help you understand how an author makes characters seem like real people.

4 **Analyzing Language in Literary Text** In literary text, analyzing language means learning new ways words can be used.

Here is a test question from a play in this unit. Even though you haven't read the play, see if you can answer the question.

What do the stage directions in this line tell a reader?

Mr. Malloy: *(Looking around the garden)* I can't believe how much work you did in just a few hours.

A the look on Mr. Malloy's face

B the tone of Mr. Malloy's voice

C the way Ms. Simon reacts

D the way Mr. Malloy moves his body

You need to know what a stage direction is in order to answer this question. The stage direction is the words in parentheses after the character's name. Match the stage direction to the answer that best describes it. If Mr. Malloy looks around, he must be moving. So, choice D is the correct answer. Although C seems like a possible answer, it is not specific, and stage directions usually tell an actor exactly what to do.

LESSON 1

Elements of a Narrative

Objectives 3.A.3.a, b, c, g

A **narrative** is usually a fiction story, one that someone has made up. Novels, short stories, mysteries, and fantasies are all fictional narratives.

Realistic Fiction is probably what you read most often. It is usually about people who could be real, often someone whose life is like yours. Books by writers such as Judy Blume and Jerry Spinelli are realistic modern fiction.

Historical Fiction can also be realistic, but it takes place in a different time. The characters in historical fiction are facing problems in another context—the revolutionary war, for example.

Science Fiction and **Fantasies** are stories that take place in a different place. A science fiction story may be about a family taking a trip to Mars. A fantasy, on the other hand, would be about a place that is not real and might include talking animals or unreal creatures. Think of the Harry Potter books.

The elements of a narrative include the characters, the plot, the setting, and the narrator, that is, the voice of the author.

Characters make the story real. An author usually describes how characters look and talk. The "talk" part is the **dialogue.**

The **plot** means the events or action in the story. Usually the events take place in chronological, or time, order. The part of the plot that makes a story exciting is the **conflict.** Sometimes the conflict is a struggle between two or more characters. Or it can involve making a big decision.

The **setting** is the time and place in which the story events take place. The time can be past, present, or future. An author uses the setting to create the **tone** or feeling of a story.

The **narrator** is the person telling the story. The narrator has a particular **point of view.** When the narrator tells the story in his or her own words, it is called first person point of view. A narrative can also be told from the third person. A character in the story may be telling the story as if he or she were reporting the events. A story can also be told by a narrator who is "unseen"—the author telling the story.

Guided Practice

Read this selection. Then answer the questions that follow.

While Dad parked our truck at the entrance to the Farmers' Market on West Fourth Street in Claremont city, I got right to work. It was only six a.m., but many of the farmers were already at their stalls. Saturday was always the busiest time of the week, especially in the summer. I taped our banner, "Sunnyside Farms," to the front of our booth. Then I helped Dad unload the truck. Soon all our homemade cheeses, breads, and cakes were on display. As we worked, our dog, Mack, watched us. I've always considered myself pretty good at reading Mack's mind. Today he seemed to say, "I'd like to help you, but I can't."

"That's okay, Mack," I said, as I patted his head. "Just having you here is enough. I bet our customers will like you."

"Just remember, Josh," Dad said. "Mack has to be on a leash at all times. That's one of the rules of the Farmers' Market. And if we don't follow them, we can't come back next week." I nodded. After all, Mack was so well behaved, that wouldn't be a problem.

Just before lunch, I decided to take Mack for a walk. Everything was fine until he saw a squirrel run up a tree. Right away, Mack had that "I want to be a squirrel" look on his face. He lunged for the tree so hard that his leash snapped off. Then Mack took off. He raced past baby strollers, under tables, and around people's legs. He even raced past a sign that said "All dogs must be on a leash in the Farmers' Market."

Finally, Mack stopped running. Unfortunately, he was right in front of Len Bennett, the manager of the Farmers' Market. He grabbed Mack's collar and looked straight at me. Then he pointed to the sign. "You know the rules of the Farmers' Market, Josh," he said sternly. "And Mack has just broken one of them. Looks like we have a problem."

What is the setting of this story?

- **A** a store on West Fourth Street
- **B** a Farmers' Market
- **C** in the country
- **D** Sunnyside Farms

The setting is the place where a story happens. The first sentence of paragraph 1 tells about Dad parking the car in the front of the Farmers' Market. So the correct answer is B.

When does the story take place?

- **A** in the afternoon
- **B** in the evening
- **C** at night
- **D** in the morning

Paragraph 1 tells you that Josh and his dad got to the market at 6 a.m. Paragraph 4 tells you that Josh took his dog for a walk just before lunch. The story takes place in the morning. So choice D is correct.

What is the point of view of this story?

- **A** first person point of view
- **B** second person point of view
- **C** third person point of view
- **D** the author's point of view

Look at paragraph 1. The narrator of the story is Josh, one of the characters. He uses the first person pronouns *I* and *we*. So choice A is correct.

What is the main conflict in the story? Explain who is having the conflict and what it is about.

____

____

____

____

____

____

Look at the last paragraph of the story. Josh loses control of Mack. Mack races past a sign that says "All dogs must be on a leash in the Farmers' Market." So, Josh is in conflict with the rules of the Farmers' Market.

Now read this story and answer the questions that follow.

The hikers heard the first growl of thunder when they reached the base of Bear Mountain. Mrs. Morgan checked her watch. "It's almost three o'clock, kids," she said. "I didn't expect a storm today. But we should make it back to camp before the rain starts. Let's keep walking."

As Mrs. Morgan and her children continued along the trail, the sky above Wilderness National Park grew dark. Suddenly, the gentle breeze became a strong wind. Fierce gusts shook the tree branches above the hikers' heads. "It feels more like winter than the beginning of May," Sarah said to her older brother, Ben. Then they took out their warm, hooded jackets from their backpacks. Their mother pointed to a stream next to the hiking trail. "That stream leads right to our camp," she said. "We're not very far from home."

Suddenly a flash of lightning lit up the sky. A few seconds later a clap of thunder roared in the distance. "Looks like that storm is getting closer," Mrs. Morgan said.

"How can you tell that, Mom?" Ben asked.

"You count the number of seconds between the lightning and the thunder. Then you divide that number by five. The answer tells you how many miles away the storm is," Mrs. Morgan answered.

In just a few seconds the sky slipped from daylight into night. The leafy trees looked threatening in the darkness. As Ben and Sarah watched, the stream was transformed into a raging river. Water splashed across the hiking trail. The strong wind almost knocked Ben and Sarah over. Walking on the slippery path was difficult. Mrs. Morgan pointed to a cabin about ten yards away. "That's a forest ranger's station. This lightning can be dangerous. We can wait out the storm in there. Let's go." A few seconds later, Sarah, Ben, and their mother were safe inside the cabin.

What is the point of view of the story narrator?

- **A** second person point of view
- **B** first person point of view
- **C** Mrs. Morgan's point of view
- **D** third person point of view

Look at the third person pronoun *she* in the first paragraph. In the second paragraph, the narrator describes what all the characters do and think. Therefore, the story is told from the third person point of view. So choice D is the correct answer.

Where does the story take place?

- **A** in Wilderness National Park
- **B** at the top of Bear Mountain
- **C** at a lakeside campsite
- **D** in a forest ranger's cabin

The first sentence of paragraph 2 describes the sky above Wilderness National Park. So choice A is the correct answer.

What is the conflict in the story?

- **A** the stream and the storm
- **B** Mrs. Morgan and her children
- **C** Ben and Sarah
- **D** the hikers and nature

Look at the description of the thunderstorm in the last paragraph. The wind is so strong that Sarah and Ben have trouble walking. The hiking path becomes slippery. The lightning is dangerous. Therefore, the conflict in the story is between the hikers and nature. So choice D is the correct answer.

Which of these is the time setting of the story?

A early in the morning

B in the middle of the afternoon

C after dark

D late at night

In the first paragraph Mrs. Morgan says that it is three o'clock in the afternoon. So choice B is the correct answer.

What does Mrs. Morgan's dialogue tell you about the kind of person she is? Give at least *two* examples to explain your answer.

____

____

____

____

____

____

Mrs. Morgan seems very calm and wise. Even though a storm is coming, she doesn't get upset. She tells the kids that a stream means they're not far from home, and she explains how to tell where the storm is by the lightning and thunder. But she is wise enough to lead them to the ranger's station.

Test Yourself

Now read this selection and answer the questions that follow.

Dana sat nervously in front of her computer. "Is it my imagination or did the screen just get bigger?" she thought. "Maybe it's because my English assignment is due tomorrow. The problem is I don't know what to write about."

Her grandmother's antique clock in the hall chimed ten o'clock. Outside her window, a half moon hung like a silver comma in the winter sky.

The house was completely silent. Dana's parents wouldn't be home for another hour. Her younger brother had gone to bed at eight o'clock. Outside her bedroom door, shadowy shapes seemed to float down the half-lit hallway. Dana's heart began to pound. She forced herself to turn back to the computer screen. "Listening to music would help, but I don't want to wake up Henry."

Dana typed one word and stopped. "Why did I put off writing this assignment until the last minute?" she thought. "I try to organize my time, but it never seems to work."

Suddenly, Dana heard a crash from the kitchen on the first floor. She crept downstairs, afraid of what she might find there. As she made her way to the kitchen, she turned on every light in the house. Then she heard a light tapping sound that seemed to grow louder and louder. Dana tried to be brave, but her legs were shaking. She forced herself to peer inside the kitchen. There was a jar of flour on the floor. The family cat, Smokey, was sitting proudly in the middle of the mess. As he licked his flour-covered paws, his tail thumped against the tile floor.

Relieved, Dana smiled at the familiar sight. Then she turned on the kitchen light. Suddenly the house was plunged into darkness. Gripping a flashlight, Dana made her way slowly down the basement stairs. When Smokey brushed against her legs, she screamed in fear. In the basement she finally found the fuse box. After replacing the blown fuse with shaking hands, Dana ran up the stairs to her bedroom. This time, Smokey was right behind her. Dana checked on Henry. He was sound asleep. She went back to her room and sat down in front of her computer screen. She typed the first sentence of her essay: "Sometimes, babysitting can be a scary experience."

1 What is the point of view of this story?

A first person point of view

B Henry's point of view

C third person point of view

D Dana's point of view

2 Where does this story take place?

A in Dana's bedroom

B in Henry's bedroom

C in the living room

D in Dana's house

3 When does this story take place?

A on a winter night

B on an autumn morning

C on a spring afternoon

D on a summer evening

4 What is one conflict in the story?

A between Dana and her fear

B between Dana and her brother

C between Dana and her cat

D between Dana and her parents

5 How do the details of the setting in this story set the tone? Give at least *three* examples of the setting.

____

____

____

____

____

____

6 Why do you think the narrator focused on Dana in the story? Explain your answer.

Plays and Poetry

Objectives 3.A.4.a, b, c, d; 3.A.5.a, b, c, d; 3.A.7.b

Plays

A **play** is a story that is performed by actors on a stage. Plays are divided into **acts** and **scenes.** An **act** is like a chapter in a book. Acts are made up of scenes, which are part of the action that take place in one location. When you watch a play in a theater or read the script of a play in a book, you will see the following elements.

Characters are the people who take part in the play's action. A list of these characters always appears at the beginning of a play or in the program. The name of the actor who takes the part of each character follows the character's name. Sometimes, there is a **narrator,** who describes events in the play to the audience or reader.

The **setting** is the time and place where the dramatic action takes place. Sometimes the setting is described in a brief **introduction** at the beginning of a play. This introduction provides the reader with background information about the characters and events in the play.

Stage directions explain how the actors should move and speak. In a script, these stage directions are usually printed in italics and set off from the dialogue and the characters' names.

Dialogue is the conversation between characters in a play. In a printed version of a play, the dialogue comes directly after the character's name. A **monologue** is a long speech spoken by one character to the audience.

Props are objects, such as books or telephones, that are used by the characters on a stage. Props are part of the **scenery,** which includes the objects and painted sets that create the setting of the play. The **lighting** refers to the brightness and types of lights used on the stage. The **props, scenery,** and **lighting** are usually described in the stage directions.

Guided Practice

Read this scene from a play. Then answer the questions that follow.

The Newcomer

By Cynthia Benjamin

The Players:

Eva Gonzalez, *a fifth grade student*	Sarah Marks
Joe Polasky, *a fifth grade student*	Larry Sellers
Lisa Connors, *a fifth grade student*	Tanya Shaw
Rob Lawrence, *a fifth grade student, just transferred to Hamilton Middle School*	Joe Cooper

ACT ONE Scene One

Eva, Joe, and Lisa enter the lunchroom of Hamilton Middle School. After buying lunch, they sit together at a table. Rob Lawrence, who has just transferred to their school, eats alone at another table.

Eva: *(Excitedly)* I can't believe summer is over and we're back in school again.

Joe: *(Sounding displeased)* Well, I can. Same old classroom. Same old lunchroom. *(He points to his plate)* And definitely the same old food. Boy, I'd give anything to be back at the pool again.

Lisa: *(Rolling her eyes)* Doing what—the doggy paddle in the shallow end?

Joe: *(Laughing)* No, a back flip off the high board. *(He smiles.)* Okay, maybe it was a dive off the junior board. But at least I didn't go in belly-first the way I did last year. *(He snaps his fingers.)* Maybe I'll write about learning to dive for my English assignment.

Eva: *(Lowering her voice, she indicates Rob Lawrence, sitting alone at another table.)* Isn't he the new kid who was in our English class this morning? He seemed really flustered when Mr. Lewinski called on him.

Joe: I heard he just transferred from Greenview Middle School. Boy, I remember what that was like. It can feel really strange being in a new school. No wonder he seemed a little shy in class.

Eva: Maybe we should ask him to have lunch with us? *(Joe gets up from the table and walks over to Rob.)*

Joe: *(To Rob)* You were in our English class this morning. Why don't you bring your lunch over to our table?

Rob: *(Shyly)* Okay, thanks. *(Rob and Joe walk back to the lunch table together. They both sit down. Rob seems uncomfortable.)*

Lisa: How do you like Hamilton so far?

Rob: *(Shrugs)* It's okay. Guess I just have to get used to it.

Eva: Are you going to join one of the sports teams?

Rob: *(Uncertain)* Well, I really love to swim.

Joe: No kidding. So do I. Were you on the team at your old school?

Rob: I was the captain. *(Modestly)* I mean, it's no big deal or anything.

Lisa: Are you kidding? Of course it is. You should talk to Coach Lim after lunch. He's always looking for good swimmers for the team.

(The stage lights dim, as the three students continue talking.)

End of ACT ONE Scene One

What does the stage direction in this line tell a reader?

Rob: *(Shyly)* Okay, thanks.

- **A** the look on Rob's face
- **B** the way Rob walks
- **C** the way Rob feels
- **D** what Rob thinks

The stage direction describes how Rob should say his line. He feels shy since he is new to the school. So choice C is the correct answer.

What is an example of a prop used in this selection?

- **A** a plate of food
- **B** Rob's clothes
- **C** the stage lighting
- **D** Eva's voice

A prop is an object used by an actor. This scene takes place in the cafeteria after the kids have bought their lunches. So choice A is correct.

What is an example of dialogue that is spoken by Eva?

- **A** "Maybe we should ask him to have lunch with us?"
- **B** "End of ACT ONE Scene One"
- **C** *"He points to his plate."*
- **D** "I heard he just transferred from Greenview Middle School."

Choice B tells the end of the scene. Choice C is a stage direction, and choice D is dialogue spoken by Joe. Choice A is the only example of dialogue spoken by Eva.

What can you tell about Joe's character from his dialogue in this scene? Give at least *two* examples.

____

____

____

____

____

Joe can make fun of himself. He says, "But at least I didn't go in belly-first the way I did last year." Also, Joe understands other people's feelings. When he talks about Rob, he says, "I heard he just transferred from Greenview Middle School. I remember what that was like."

Test Yourself

Now read this scene from a play and answer the questions that follow.

The Jefferson Street Garden

By Larry Summers

The Players:

Narrator	Jim Hale
Ms. Simon, *a fifth grade teacher*	Rachel Smith
Louis Zelig, *a fifth grade student*	Ramon Garcia
Maggie Tucker, *a fifth grade student*	Deirdre Todd
Tina Rogers, *a fifth grade student*	Rena Smith
Mr. Malloy, *a resident of Jefferson Street*	Jerry Toney
Tim Waters, *a newspaper reporter*	Robert Snyder
Jesse, Jim, Cynthia, Elle, *all fifth grade students*	

ACT ONE Scene One

Ms. Simon and her fifth grade class enter the Jefferson Street Community Garden. They are greeted by Mr. Malloy, the president of the Jefferson Street Block Association. It's Saturday morning. Several of the students carry plants, potting soil, and shovels. Mr. Malloy turns on a hose and begins watering some of the plants.

Narrator: It's planting day at the Jefferson Street Community Garden. Ms. Simon's fifth grade class has just arrived to help plant new trees and plants. It's a Saturday morning in April.

Ms. Simon: *(Looking around)* Okay, everyone. Remember what we talked about in science class yesterday. Remember to cover the young plants completely with dirt before watering them.

Tina: *(Excitedly)* Don't worry, Ms. Simon. This is going to be the best community garden in the city.

Mr. Malloy: Thank you for your help everyone. Let's get to work.

(The stage lights dim as the students begin to plant. The narrator steps forward.)

Narrator: The student volunteers worked in the community garden all morning. Then they stopped to have lunch.

(The stage lights grow brighter. The students are sitting on benches in the garden. They are eating sandwiches. Mr. Malloy walks into the garden.)

Mr. Malloy: *(Looking around the garden)* I can't believe how much work you did in just a few hours.

Tina: We organized everything before we came. I asked businesses in the neighborhood to donate the plants.

Louis: *(Smiling)* And my dad gave us a tree from his nursery.

Ms. Simon: *(To Mr. Malloy)* Everyone in the community wanted to help. This garden is important to all of us.

Mr. Malloy: *(Becoming serious)* I'm afraid I have some upsetting news. I've just found out the city is considering selling this land.

All the students: *(At the same time)* Why? What for?

Mr. Malloy: So a garage can be built here. There isn't enough space for parking in this neighborhood.

Maggie: *(Very determined)* But a garden is important, too.

Mr. Malloy: I couldn't agree with you more. *(As he speaks, Tim Waters walks onstage.)* That's why I invited Tim Waters to talk to you. He's a reporter from the Jefferson *Bulletin.*

Tim Waters: *(Taking out his notebook)* I'd like to ask all of you why planting this garden is so important. *(Pointing to Maggie)* Why don't you go first?

(The stage lights dim.) **End of ACT ONE Scene One**

1 What is an example of something the narrator says in this selection?

- **A** "ACT ONE Scene One"
- **B** "It's planting day at the Jefferson Community Garden."
- **C** "I'm afraid I have some upsetting news."
- **D** "We organized everything before we came."

2 What is the name of the newspaper reporter in this scene?

- **A** Ms. Simon
- **B** Mr. Malloy
- **C** Tim Waters
- **D** Maggie Tucker

3 What do you learn by reading the introduction to the scene?

A the title of the play

B the names of the characters

C what happens in Act Two

D the setting of the play

4 What do the stage directions in this line tell a reader?

Mr. Malloy: *(Looking around the garden)* I can't believe how much work you did in just a few hours.

A the look on Mr. Malloy's face

B the tone of Mr. Malloy's voice

C the way Ms. Simon reacts

D the way Mr. Malloy moves his body

5 Think about what the characters said and did in this selection. What can readers expect they will do after learning about the city's plans for the garden?

____

____

____

____

____

____

6 How is the stage lighting used in this scene? Explain where that information can be found.

____

____

____

____

____

____

Poetry

Poetry uses musical language to create word pictures and sound effects in your mind. As you read a poem, think about these important elements.

Repeating sounds at the end of words is called **rhyme.** Sometimes the rhyme comes at the end of a line of poetry:

I watched the trees

Dancing in the breeze.

Sometimes the rhyming words appear in the same line:

The thrilling, chilling sounds of the night.

Rhythm is the pattern of stressed and unstressed beats or syllables in a line of poetry. A stressed beat has more force than an unstressed beat.

Alliteration is the repetition of the same, or very similar, beginning consonant sound in words in a line of poetry: For example, in "the tinkling, twinkling star" the *t* sound is an example of alliteration.

Haiku is a form of Japanese poetry with three lines. The first and third lines of a haiku have five syllables. The second line has seven syllables. Haiku creates a clear, vivid picture of an action or emotion by using images from nature.

In a **form** or **shape poem,** words are arranged on the page in the shape of a real object, such as a star or a flower. This object is what the poet is writing about in the poem.

Guided Practice

Read these poems now. Then answer the questions that follow.

The Ball

By Cynthia Benjamin

1 Look. A ball.
2 Flies fast and very, very far.
3 So swiftly that no one stops its flight.
4 It seems to soar before hitting the highest star.
5 We watch in wonder, now willing it onward.
6 The perfect sphere, it is carrying all our hopes
7 And dreams to a place beyond our reach.
8 Twirling, swirling, in the sleek night air.
9 Twisting, turning, twirling down.
10 Now slamming against earth.
11 The dream sphere is just
12 A ball. Look.

Dew Drops (A Haiku)

Dew drops on flowers.
Fall gently to the dry earth.
Silent tears of joy.

In which lines in the first poem does the poet purposely repeat the beginning sound of words?

A lines 6, 7, and 12

B lines 2, 5, and 9

C lines 1 and 4

D lines 11 and 12

The beginning sound *f* is repeated in line 2; the beginning sound *w* is repeated in line 5, and the beginning sound *t* is repeated in line 9. So B is the correct choice.

What does the poet compare the dew drops to in the second poem?

A flowers

B happiness

C tears

D earth

The dew drops in line 1 are compared to silent tears of joy in line 3. So choice C is the correct answer.

In the first poem, which word in line 4 rhymes with the last word in line 2?

A soar

B hitting

C highest

D star

The last word in line 2 is *far.* The only word that rhymes with it from line 4 is *star*. So choice D is the correct answer.

How would you describe the relationship between the shape of the first poem and its subject?

____

____

____

____

____

The poem is shaped like a ball. The subject of the poem is a ball that soars high in the sky before coming down to earth. The author arranges the words of the poem into the shape of the poem's subject to create a more dramatic effect for the descriptions.

Test Yourself

Now read these poems and answer the questions that follow.

Out of the Morning

Emily Dickinson

1 Will there really be a morning?
2 Is there such a thing as day?
3 Could I see it from the mountains
4 If I were as tall as they?

5 Has it feet like water-lilies?
6 Has it feathers like a bird?
7 Is it brought from famous countries
8 Of which I have never heard?

9 O, some scholar! Oh, some sailor!
10 Oh, some wise man from the skies!
11 Please do tell a little pilgrim
12 Where the place called morning lies!

The Storm

Thunder cracks, then dies.
Thick black clouds blanket the sky.
Rain stings my window.

1 How can you tell "The Storm" is a haiku?

A by counting the number of short vowel sounds
B by counting the number of consonant sounds
C by counting the number of syllables in each line
D by counting the number of words in the poem

2 Read the first four lines of "Out of the Morning." How would you describe the rhythm of each line?

A two unstressed beats are followed by three stressed beats
B an unstressed beat is followed by a stressed beat
C two stressed beats are followed by two unstressed beats
D a stressed beat is followed by an unstressed beat

3 Why does the speaker of the first poem refer to herself as a "pilgrim" in line 11?

A She is celebrating a new season.

B She is on an important journey to find the answer to her question.

C She is a teacher who is writing about nature.

D She is a student of the natural world.

4 What is the meaning of the word "blanket" in the second poem?

A to cover

B to cool

C to light

D to carry

5 Poets often use words such as *sizzle* or *slosh* because these words sound like what they mean. Find a word that sounds like its meaning in the second poem. Tell what the poet wanted to show by using the word.

____

____

____

____

____

____

6 What is the subject of each poem? Explain your answer using details from the poems.

____

____

____

____

____

____

Analyzing Character

Objectives 3.A.3.d, e, f

Characters are the people in stories. They can be fictional or real, such as people from history. Characters make stories interesting. You can read a story full of action and suspense, but if you don't care about the characters, chances are you won't care about much else in the story. And if you do care about the characters, it is probably because they are like real people. You judge or analyze a character from what the author tells you. How does the character talk and act? How does the character handle problems? What other characters say helps you understand a character, too. Characters change and grow in a story or book—just like real people.

Analyzing Character

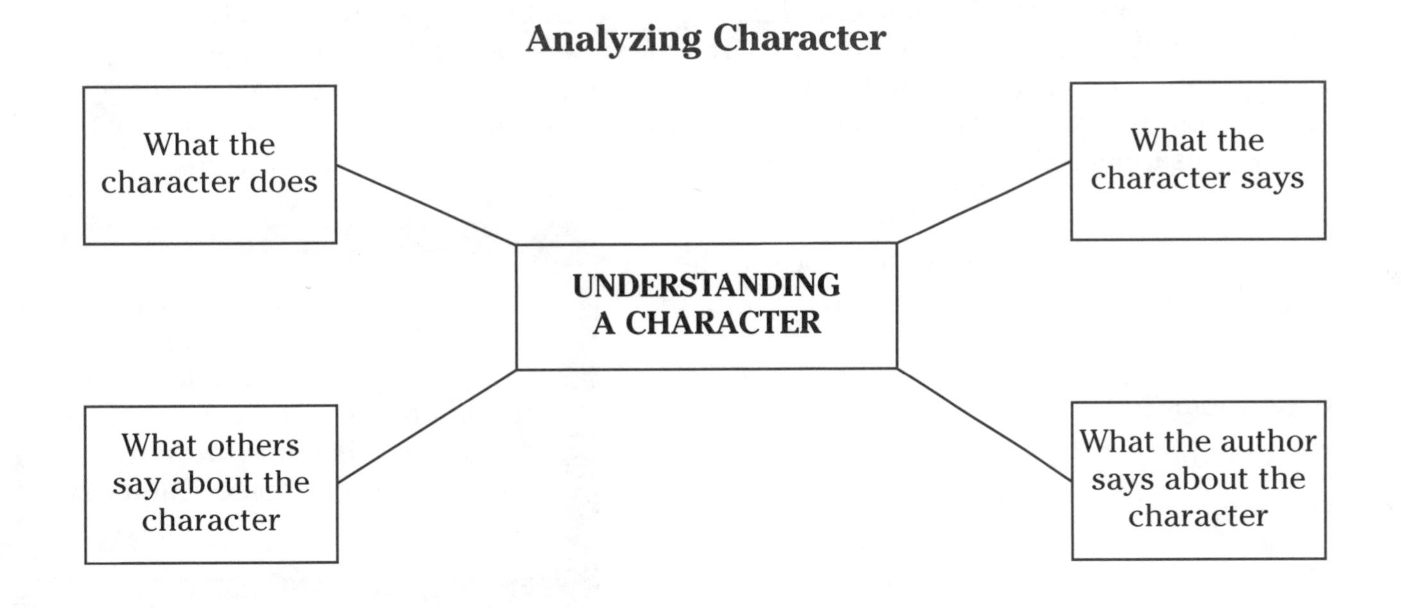

Guided Practice

Read this fable from Africa. Then answer the questions.

An ant was running around one day, looking for food. He saw a cocoon hanging from a twig. Never having seen a cocoon before, the ant stopped to take a look. When he saw something in the cocoon move its tail, he realized it was alive. "Poor creature!" said the ant. "I don't know what kind of animal you are, but I pity you. I can run anywhere I want. I can even climb to the tops of trees if that is my wish. But you are trapped in your shell, and can only move your tail a little."

The insect in the cocoon was too busy changing to reply. But a few days later, the ant came that way again. A broken shell was all that remained of the cocoon. The ant stared, wondering what had happened. Just then, he felt a cool breeze above him. He looked up and saw a beautiful butterfly fanning him with his wings. "So you pity me, do you?" said the butterfly. "Tell me now about climbing trees, as long as you can get me to listen." And the butterfly rose into the air and was soon lost from sight. The ant watched him until he disappeared.

The ant pauses in his hunt for food to look at the cocoon. This indicates that the ant was ______.

A lazy

B curious

C friendly

D hungry

The third sentence of the story tells you why the ant stopped: he had never seen a cocoon before. The word *curious* describes this behavior better than any other choice. Choice B is correct.

The ant said that he pitied the animal in the cocoon. Which of these describes his real feelings?

A He thought that the animal in the cocoon was deaf and dumb.

B He felt he was better in many ways than the animal in the cocoon.

C He wanted to be like the animal in the cocoon.

D He was hoping to become a friend of the animal in the cocoon.

The fable doesn't say what the ant is feeling, but you can tell from his words. He describes the things he can do—run and climb. The ant seems to believe his life is better than that of the animal in the cocoon. So choice B is correct.

Which of these *best* describes how the butterfly feels?

- **A** The butterfly is grateful to the ant.
- **B** The butterfly does not like being pitied.
- **C** The butterfly wants to get even with the ant.
- **D** The butterfly wants to be like the ant.

The butterfly cannot believe he is pitied by the ant, since he knows he can do much more than the ant thought he could. The fact that he flies away shows he does not like to be pitied. So choice B is correct. There is no evidence for the other choices.

How do you think the ant feels at the end of the story? Give evidence from the story to support your answer.

____

____

____

____

____

After all that happened, the ant felt embarrassed. He must have known that he made a mistake in thinking he was so superior and then saying it out loud. Meanwhile, the butterfly could do a lot more than the ant, and the ant knew it.

Read this tale about a young man who helps the poor. Then answer the questions.

How Robin Hood Became an Outlaw

An English Tale

You may have heard about the outlaw Robin Hood. He lived long ago. Storytellers say that Robin Hood stole from the rich and gave to the poor. They say that he led a band of other outlaws and lived in Sherwood Forest.

Well, outlaws are not born. They are made. Here is the story of how young Robin came to live outside the law.

Robin was a comely lad, handsome and fair. He was as bold as any young man of 18 years. And he was more. His strong arm and sharp eye had made him an excellent archer. Few were as good as he with a bow and arrow.

And so when the Sheriff of Nottingham declared an archery contest, Robin set off. He was going to win the prize of 40 marks!

Robin traveled through the Sherwood Forest to get to the contest. He walked with his bow slung over his shoulder and a quiver of arrows on his back. It was a fine day, and he whistled while he walked.

Presently, Robin came upon a group of men. They were sitting in a clearing, eating and drinking. One of the men looked up and saw Robin. "Hey, lad!" he called with his mouth still full of food. "Where are you going with that little bow and those penny arrows?"

Robin stopped and faced the man, who was still chewing. "My bow and arrows are as good as yours," Robin said. He noticed a tree standing alone in the meadow far from the group. "I will bet you 20 marks that I can hit that tree."

The men laughed at Robin. He began to get angry. Looking around, he saw a herd of deer grazing in the meadow beyond the tree. He turned to the men again. "Do you see those deer yonder? I will bet you 20 marks that I can hit the best hart among them."

The man who had first spoken stood up. Wiping his mouth with his sleeve, he laughed once more. "All right, my lad," he said. "I will bet you 20 marks that you cannot hit that hart."

Robin drew an arrow from his quiver and held it far back in his bow. Carefully, he aimed at the deer. With a zing, he let the arrow fly.

Everyone turned to watch as Robin's arrow flew straight and true. It hit the most noble hart in the herd. Robin turned to the men. "Ha!" he cried. "How did you like that shot, dear fellow?"

The man did not like it at all. Neither did his friends. They did not like to be bested by such a young man.

"Get out of here at once!" shouted the man. "You have killed one of the king's deer. By the laws of this land, your ears should be shaved close to your head!"

Looking hard at the man, Robin turned to go. He knew that the man would not pay on his bet. Suddenly, an arrow whizzed by Robin's ear. The man had shot at him!

Robin grabbed an arrow from his quiver as he spun around. He quickly fit it into his bow and let it go. The arrow flew straight at the man's heart, and he fell down dead.

Before the others could act, Robin ran. "What a terrible thing," thought Robin. "I have taken another man's life!" Robin was full of sorrow and regret. He finally sat to rest on a log far from where he had started. He knew that the king would have him killed. He knew that he must hide.

And Robin was right. The king declared him to be an outlaw. There was a reward of 200 pounds for anyone who caught him. Robin spent one long year in the woods thinking about his crime.

After some months had passed, Robin met other men like himself. They were not really bad. But they had done something that made them have to live outside of their villages.

Together, the men agreed to their own laws. They would live together in peace in the forest. They would not hurt anyone. But they would go into towns and take from the rich. They would only rob people who had become rich by being unfair to poor people. Then, Robin and his band would give the money to the poor.

Soon Robin had 100 men with him. They became known throughout the land. They were feared by evil people and loved by the good. Poor people knew that if they needed food, they could come to Robin Hood and he would give it.

Many adventures followed in Robin Hood's long life. But now you know the story of how he came to be an outlaw and rule the forest.

When Robin Hood first entered Sherwood Forest, "he whistled while he walked." He probably felt ______.

- **A** sad
- **B** confused
- **C** cheerful
- **D** angry

In the beginning of the story, Robin Hood was an excellent archer who was on his way to enter a contest. It was a nice day and nothing bad had happened yet. These descriptions and the fact that he was whistling tell you that he was content and cheerful. So choice C is correct.

How do you think Robin Hood felt after the killing? Give evidence from the tale to support your answer.

____

____

____

____

____

Both the picture on page 170 and the sentence, "Robin was full of sorrow and regret," tell that he felt terrible about what he had done and wished it hadn't happened.

Poor people came to Robin to get food. This tells you that he was ______.

A an excellent archer

B quick to lose his temper

C kind and generous

D not the leader of the band

Choices A, B, and D do not really have anything to do with people getting food from Robin. Someone who gives away food, money, or gifts of any kind to help less fortunate people could be described as kind and generous. So choice C is correct.

The author says, "Well, outlaws are not born. They are made." Is this true of Robin Hood? Explain your answer using at least *two* details from the story.

____

____

____

____

____

____

You may agree with the author's statement that no one is born a criminal, but events and choices can make one so. Robin Hood was a confident and handsome boy who wanted to enter the Sheriff of Nottingham's archery contest. Unfortunately, he met up with a group of men who made fun of him. When Robin Hood became angry, he made a bad choice to shoot a deer, which just happened to belong to the king. He made a second bad decision to shoot at the man instead of running away. He regretted his decisions, but felt his only solution was to become an outlaw.

Test Yourself

Read a passage about two friends. Then answer the questions.

Chris Henry was at the playground. He was shooting baskets at a hoop on one end of the court. I rode my bike over and watched him. He lifted his eyes, nodded at me, and sank a jump shot. I waited for him to ask me to join him. He didn't. He just went on playing one-on-one with his shadow until I asked him. "Sure, come on," he said. He tossed me the basketball.

That about matched the longest conversation we ever had. Chris had been in my class last year, but I didn't know him. He usually ate lunch by himself and didn't hang around after school. He wasn't one of those strange kids who give you an uncomfortable feeling. He just didn't go out of his way to be friendly.

Chris was one of the tallest kids in our class, but he wasn't quick. He was all knees and elbows and long, skinny arms. Still, it was hard to get around him. Every time I tried a move, his hand was in my face. He had a surprisingly smooth hook shot I couldn't have blocked with a stepladder. He must have sunk two shots for every one of mine. It was a hot July day, and after half an hour I could have mopped up the court with my t-shirt.

That was when he looked at his watch. "Got to get home," he said. "We live around the corner. You want some lemonade?"

"Sure," I said. It had been a long month since school let out. Summer was great, but it was good to have found someone who wasn't away.

I saw right off that Chris's house was full of music. There was a big piano in the living room, and music stands and music were scattered around. "You play an instrument?" I asked.

"Violin." He looked at me over his lemonade glass. "Uh, Nick, I have to practice. That's why I had to come home. If it doesn't seem too weird, you can hang here till I'm done. Read a book or watch TV. Then we can go out and do something, okay?"

It was cool and comfortable in Chris's house. "Sure, that's okay," I said. "What if I just watch you play?"

"That'd be all right," he said.

I did not know anyone who played the violin. I did not know anyone my age who played *any* instrument—I mean, seriously played one. I couldn't tell whether he was good. But when he took that violin out of his case, a change came over him. It was just him and his instrument. I might as well not have been there. I'd never seen anyone give such total attention to anything.

1 Which of these phrases does *not* contribute to a reader's picture of Chris?

2 At the beginning of the passage, Nick would most likely describe Chris as ______.

A unfriendly

B strange

C quiet

D selfish

3 Which of these *best* describes how Nick is feeling at the beginning of the passage?

A full of energy

B bored and lonely

C tired and unhappy

D angry at Chris

4 What is a conclusion readers can draw from this passage about Chris?

A He doesn't do much other than play basketball.

B He is anxious to fit in with the other kids at school.

C He practices the violin only because his parents make him.

D He can be friendly when someone is friendly to him.

5 How does Nick feel about Chris at the end of the story? Give at least *two* details from the story to support your answer.

____

____

____

____

____

____

6 Chris is very dedicated and comfortable with his violin playing. Give at least *two* examples from the story that support this statement.

____

____

____

____

____

____

LESSON 4

Analyzing Language in Literary Text

Objectives 3.A.7.b, c, d

A writer chooses words and language to set the **tone** of a story, play, or poem. The tone is the mood or feeling you get about the characters and the place. If a story begins with a dark room, a howling wind, and a creaking door, you know the writer wants you to be scared.

Writers also use **figures of speech** to help you picture or feel what is happening. Here are five figures of speech.

You have studied one figure of speech, **idioms.** An idiom is a phrase that has a meaning separate from the words in the phrase. You might read, "Bart counted to ten so he wouldn't blow his top." *Blow his top* is an idiom; it means to get very angry and yell. The writer is comparing how Bart might look and sound with the top blowing off something.

Another figure of speech is **onomatopoeia.** You are using onomatopoeia when you make a noise to imitate the sound of something. Writers use it to give readers a sense or feeling. "The wind whished by my ears as I zoomed down the hill." The words "whished" and "zoomed" sound like what is happening.

When you say that a pillow is "as hard as a rock," you are using a **simile.** A simile compares two things that are very different using the words *like* or *as.* "The wind tapped like a tired man" is a simile from a poem.

If you compare two things but don't use the words *like* or *as,* you are using a **metaphor.** "It's raining cats and dogs" is a metaphor. It says to you that the rain is coming down so hard it seems as heavy as animals. "A waterfall of leaves spilled from the tree" is another metaphor. It compares falling leaves to water.

Personification is another kind of comparison. That means a writer *personifies* something that is not human, or makes it like a person. "The wind tapped like a tired man" is also an example of personification. "A breeze sang through the trees" is another example of personification.

Guided Practice

Read this story. Then answer the following questions.

The Scary Adventure

My best friend Cole and I often talked about it. We always said we were going to go into the old house where no one lived any more. One day Cole said to me, "You are just chicken. You are afraid to go into the old house."

"Are you kidding?" I asked. "Are you pulling my leg? I'll go in any time."

"Let's go now," said Cole. So we went.

We climbed the rickety front porch steps. The porch floor creaked as we walked across it. "After you," Cole said when we got to the front door.

"No, you go first," I said to him.

"Let's talk about this," said Cole.

So we sat down in front of the door. I don't know why, but my mom came to my mind. I could just hear her saying, "You are in hot water now. You are in big trouble. I told you never to go into an empty house. You could get hurt. There could be a big hole on the other side of the door. You could fall through it." My mom has a wild imagination.

Cole said, "What if there is a big hole on the other side of the door? We could fall down into it."

"I can't believe it," I said. "It's like you are reading my mind. I was just thinking the same thing."

"We could fall into it," Cole repeated. "It might be a slimy pit filled with bugs and snakes. An old robber with one eye, who is hiding in the house, might find us. He might throw a pot of boiling swamp water on our heads."

"And rotten eggs on top of that," I said. We were both shivering with fear by now.

"Let's get out of here," yelled Cole.

We ran like the wind until we reached my yard. "That was a close call," said Cole.

"You can say that again," I said.

"That was a close call," said Cole.

"I didn't mean for you to repeat that," I said. "It's just an expression."

"I knew that," said Cole. "I was just trying to be funny."

In sentence 3, the word *chicken* means ______.

A rickety

B afraid

C silly

D creaked

The word *chicken* can have more than one meaning. In this case it is used to mean that someone is afraid. So choice B is correct.

If someone tells you that you are in hot water, what does that person mean?

____

____

____

____

____

That person does not mean that you are actually standing in hot water. The person is using an idiom. Here, "in hot water" means "being in trouble." The person is telling you that you are in trouble for something.

What does the author compare the boys running to?

A rotten eggs

B a close call

C the wind

D bugs and snakes

Similes compare two things using *like* or *as*. In this case, the author tells you that the boys "ran like the wind" to reach the yard. So choice C is correct.

Which sentence means the same as "Are you pulling my leg?"

A Are you hurting me?

B Are you teasing me?

C Are you tripping me?

D Are you scaring me?

Choice B is the correct answer. "Are you kidding?" is the sentence before "Are you pulling my leg?" This gives you a clue that this expression means the same as "Are you teasing me?"

What type of figurative language is used in this sentence from the selection?

The porch floor creaked as we walked across it.

A onomatopoeia

B simile

C metaphor

D personification

Similes and metaphors are used to compare two things. So choices B and C are not correct. Personification gives things the characteristics of a person. So choice D is not correct either. Onomatopoeia uses a word that sounds like what it means. You can probably imagine the floor creaking because the word *creak* sounds like what it means. So choice A is correct.

Read this poem about in-line skates. Then answer the questions that follow.

In-Line Skates

by Azula Gallego

Slicing through the wind like a knife, I push and glide,
Push and glide, to the top of Rankin Street,
Then down, crouching, dropping like a stone in a well.
Each bump is a rocket launcher, hurtling me into space
For the briefest moment, before I land, arms out for balance
As graceful as a dancer, as look-at-me as any peacock—
—in my imagination.

Christmas is a far-off planet,
My birthday an unimaginably distant star.
I ask you, am I out of line
For wanting in-line skates?

Which of these phrases is a metaphor?

- **A** Christmas is a far-off planet
- **B** as graceful as a dancer
- **C** arms out for balance
- **D** dropping like a stone in a well

A metaphor is a comparison. Three of the choices make comparisons: choices A, B, and D. But a metaphor does not use the words *like* or *as*. So you can eliminate choices B and D. But choice A, "Christmas is a far-off planet" is a metaphor.

The simile "as look-at-me as any peacock" means that the skater is ______.

- **A** showing off
- **B** flying like a bird
- **C** looking in the mirror
- **D** going even faster

Why would a person compare himself or herself to a peacock? A peacock is a bird that likes to show off its colorful feathers to get attention. By comparing herself to a peacock, the author means she is showing off and wants other people to notice. Choice A is correct.

Which of these phrases is an idiom?

- **A** push and glide
- **B** the briefest moment
- **C** in my imagination
- **D** out of line

The separate words in an idiom do not mean the same thing as the words together. All the answer choices are words from the poem. Is there anything different about them? Of these choices the only one where the words are used differently is "out of line" (Choice D). You can see that in this poem "out of line" does not have anything to do with standing on line or going in a straight line. These meanings do not make sense in this poem. Here "out of line" means "being wrong" or "breaking a rule." The author is asking whether it's wrong to want a pair of in-line skates. Choice D is correct.

Explain the meaning of the phrase "Slicing through the wind like a knife" and explain what kind of figure of speech it is.

____

____

____

____

____

The author uses the simile "like a knife" to compare her speed to a knife cutting through the wind while skating. You can picture her steadily skating with her head pushed forward trying to get to the top of the street.

Test Yourself

Read this selection from a story. Then answer the questions that follow.

I had a ball that summer. My aunt and uncle had rented a house at Canada Lake. They invited me to join them for a month. In August our apartment is like an oven. I fell all over myself saying yes.

The back door of the house had a small door cut out of the bottom. It was for a cat to get in and out. My cousins had a cat called Rudy. He was a tough street-kid of a cat. He had a patch of black fur around one eye that made him look like a pirate. Rudy sometimes came up to you, like a puppy, expecting to be petted. Other times he'd disappear for a day or two. He'd come back a four-legged bush, with bits of leaves and bark sticking to his fur.

At night the house was spooky. Everyone in my cousins' family sleeps like a log. I'd often wake up during the night. It was completely quiet. There was a big old maple tree out front. Its roots made camel humps in the grass, and its leaves brushed against my window.

One night I was feeling a little out of sorts. I went to bed early. I woke up with a dream of howling. At least I thought it was a dream at first. It took me a while to understand what I was hearing. It was Rudy, howling out front. Then I realized it wasn't one cat, it was two, no—a lot of cats. It was very quiet, like conversation. Then I knew that they weren't outside. They were in the house.

I tiptoed downstairs. There were seven cats in a circle on the living room rug. I recognized Rudy and a couple of others I had seen on the street. A club meeting of cats. I don't know whether they were discussing something serious or just telling jokes.

They didn't stick around long. Maybe I made a noise. In any case, one of them snarled. Then they took off like a 50-meter dash for the cat door, all except Rudy. He just stood there licking his paws, paying no attention to me.

I went back upstairs to bed. In the morning, I kept it all to myself. It seemed a special favor that I had seen it.

1 The idiom "I fell all over myself" means ______.

A I was so excited I couldn't stand still.

B I was clumsy and tripped over my feet.

C I had a wonderful time.

D I wasn't sure I wanted to go.

2 The narrator compares his family's apartment to ______.

A an oven

B heat

C August

D a ball

3 Which of these is *not* a figure of speech that helps you picture Rudy?

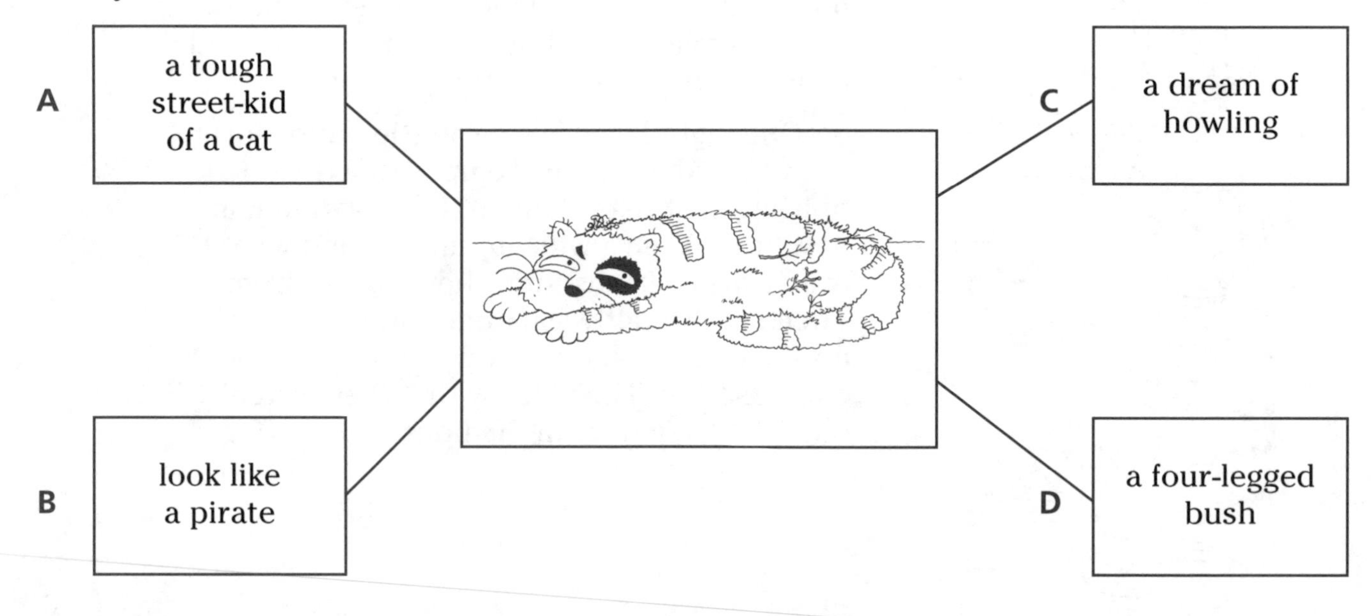

4 Which of these phrases is a metaphor?

- **A** Rudy howling out front
- **B** my cousins' family sleeps like logs
- **C** feeling a little out of sorts
- **D** a club meeting of cats

5 What does the narrator compare to "camel humps"?

- **A** the shadows of the leaves
- **B** the roots of the maple tree
- **C** birds flying by his window
- **D** the cats sitting in a circle

6 Explain the meaning of the phrase "took off like a 50-meter dash" as it is used in the story.

____

____

____

____

____

____

Guided Test

Choose the word or group of words that means the same, or almost the same, as the underlined word. Then mark the space for your answer choice.

SAMPLE

To <u>attempt</u> means to ______.

A see

B try

C want

D know

HINT

With this type of question, sometimes, you either know it or you don't. You should think very hard to see if you can remember hearing the vocabulary words. You can also look for clues in the words.

1 An <u>emotion</u> is a ______.

A song

B party

C feeling

D belief

HINT

You've heard people talk about being <u>emotional</u>. It usually means they are very sad or very happy.

2 <u>Transparent</u> means ______.

A new

B clear

C brittle

D terrible

HINT

The prefix *trans-* means across or through. Think about <u>trans</u>portation (to carry something from one place to another). If something is <u>transparent</u>, you can see through it.

3 To <u>resign</u> means to ______.

A quit

B write

C arrive

D improve

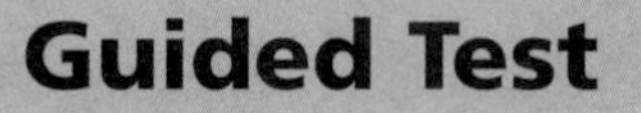

4 Amy runs three miles every day.

In which sentence is the word runs used to mean the same thing that it means in the sentence above?

> **HINT**
>
> For this kind of question, ask yourself what the underlined word actually means in each sentence. Try to replace it with a different word or phrase. In the boxed sentence, when Amy runs, she *moves quickly on foot*.

A My baseball team scored two runs to win the game.

B The window shade was old, and it had many runs in it.

C A dog runs around in circles in the park.

D The school runs through a box of paper every day.

5 Jake wore a cap on his head.

In which sentence is the word head used to mean the same thing that it means in the sentence above?

A Cara bumped her head.

B Lenny was at the head of the line.

C Mr. Quinn is the head librarian.

D Jackson has a good head for numbers.

Read the first sentence. Use the other words in the sentence to help you figure out the meaning of the underlined word. Then mark the space for your answer choice.

6 The hapless man slipped on the ice, spilled all his groceries, and twisted his ankle. Hapless means ______.

A athletic

B mature

C determined

D unfortunate

> **HINT**
>
> If all those bad things happened to you, which word would best describe you?

7 Lillian transposed the letter from print to script. Transposed means ______.

A held

B read

C copied

D mailed

8 The clever detective was able to <u>thwart</u> the plans of the sneaky thieves. <u>Thwart</u> means ______.

A copy

B spoil

C follow

D improve

Our National Anthem

by Cornelia York

You know the song. You've heard it many times. You may have heard someone sing it before a professional sports game. You may have sung it with classmates in school. The song is "The Star-Spangled Banner." It is our national anthem.

During the War of 1812, the British and Americans fought a kind of rematch of the Revolutionary War. In 1814, British soldiers caught an American named William Beanes. They held him prisoner on a ship in Chesapeake Bay. General John Mason was in charge of prisoner exchanges for the U.S. He sent two Americans to bargain with the British to have Beanes set free. One of these was Francis Scott Key, a friend of Beanes.

The two Americans traveled to Baltimore. They boarded a flag of truce ship. This was a ship on which soldiers from both sides could negotiate without fear of bloodshed. The truce ship took Francis Scott Key to the British battleship just as the British were getting ready to bomb Fort McHenry, an important fort near Baltimore Harbor. The British were ready to release Beanes, but they could not let the Americans go right away. They were afraid the men would warn the fort about the bombardment. They forced the Americans to remain on the flag of truce ship until the battle was over.

HINT

On a reading test, some selections are fiction, but this one is true. You might already know about this song and how it came to be written. If you do, your knowledge can help you. If you do not know, don't worry. Everything you will need to answer the questions is right here.

The bombing began on September 13, 1814. It lasted all day and most of the night. Francis Scott Key and his companions were worried about the fort. The men walked back and forth on the ship's deck. They tried to see the fort through the darkness. Each time a bomb exploded, they caught a brief flash of the fort. When the dawn finally came, they were thrilled to see an American flag still flying above the fort.

Francis Scott Key was so impressed that he started writing the verses to a song. The song told of the events he had just seen. Soon the British released the prisoners, and they returned to Baltimore. As soon as he could, Key finished writing the song.

The melody came from a well-known song by John Stafford Smith. The lyrics begin with the famous line, "O, say can you see, by the dawn's early light, what so proudly we hailed, at the twilight's last gleaming?" The song was a tremendous hit. Beginning in 1895, U.S. Army soldiers sang it when they raised and lowered the flag. However, it did not become our national anthem until Congress approved it in 1931. Today, the U.S. flag flies over the grave of Francis Scott Key, which is located in Frederick, Maryland.

9 This article is mainly about a famous ______.

A war

B song

C battle

D person

HINT

The article is about all of these things, but which is it *mainly* about? Look at the title and read the first paragraph again.

10 The author's main purpose in writing this article is to ______.

A tell the history of "The Star-Spangled Banner"

B describe the battle scene at Fort McHenry

C give directions to the grave of Francis Scott Key

D persuade readers to sing the national anthem

11 What does the word *negotiate* mean?

This was a ship on which soldiers from both sides could *negotiate* without fear of bloodshed.

A sail and relax

B spy and trick

C meet and fight

D talk and bargain

HINT

Why were the men meeting on this ship? What was their purpose? Read paragraph 3 again.

12 To keep Francis Scott Key from warning the Americans about the battle, the British ______.

A kept him on the ship until the battle was over

B agreed to release William Beanes to him

C made him stay on the ship's deck all night

D held him prisoner on a ship in the Chesapeake Bay

HINT

Look for a problem and a solution to the problem.

13 Which sentence in paragraph 6 states an opinion?

- **A** "The melody came from a song by John Stafford Smith."
- **B** "The song was a tremendous hit."
- **C** "U.S. Army soldiers sang it when they raised and lowered the flag."
- **D** "Today, the U.S. flag flies over the grave of Francis Scott Key."

> **HINT**
>
> **Words such as "awful," "delicious," and "talented" signal an opinion. They are not based on facts that can be checked.**

14 Which happened *first?*

- **A** Francis Scott Key traveled to Baltimore.
- **B** The British began to bomb Fort McHenry.
- **C** William Beanes was taken prisoner by the British.
- **D** Congress made "The Star-Spangled Banner" our national anthem.

15 Write a summary of this article in your own words. Be sure to include at least *three* important ideas from the article.

____

____

____

____

____

____

16 Explain where these words come from, what they mean, and why they are important.

"O, say can you see, by the dawn's early light, what so proudly we hailed, at the twilight's last gleaming?"

> **HINT**
>
> **You already know part of the answer. To get a top score, be sure to answer all parts of the question.**

____

____

____

____

____

____

Stray Cat

by Judith Lipsett

1 I'd like to introduce my cat—
I found her one cold day.
Her scraggly fur and muddy tail
Told me she was a stray.
5 And yet the look within her eyes
Said, *Won't you let me stay?*

I opened up a tuna can
And put some in a dish,
And then I sat down quietly
10 To watch her eat that fish.
And still the look within her eyes
Said, *Won't you grant my wish?*

At first she didn't eat a bite—
She was afraid to try.
15 But soon her hunger was so strong
That she could not be shy.
And now the look within her eyes
Said, *Must we say good-bye?*

When every bit of fish was gone,
20 She came right up to me
And rubbed her face against my leg,
Then climbed upon my knee.
I said, *I guess you're my cat now.*
Her purr said, *I agree.*

HINT

On a reading test, you will find some selections that are fiction and some that are nonfiction. Examples of fiction include stories, poems, or dramas. This selection is a poem. When you first read a poem, read to understand what it is about. Later, you can go back and look for specific words, rhymes, and examples of figurative language.

17 How did the cat probably feel in lines 2–14 of the poem?

A angry

B pleased

C scared

D wonderful

HINT

The cat was cold and hungry and still afraid to take tuna fish from the speaker.

18 Readers can tell this selection is a poem because it includes ______.

A the voice of a speaker

B a cute animal character

C a conflict that gets solved

D repeated words and rhyming lines

HINT

Which answer is usually found *only* in poems?

19 What does the word *scraggly* mean in the sentence below?

Her *scraggly* fur and muddy tail/Told me she was a stray.

A clean
B rough
C combed
D trimmed

HINT

A stray cat would not have an owner to wash, comb, or trim the hair on its coat and tail.

20 Which words *best* fit the speaker in the poem?

A sad and lonely
B mean and nasty
C wise and clever
D kind and loving

HINT

The first two choices sound bad. The poem sounded good, so it is probably not one of these.

21 At the end of each stanza, how does the poet show what the cat and the narrator say to each other?

A by using italic type
B by underlining words
C by using large, bold type
D by using quotation marks.

HINT

Look back at the poem to answer this question.

22 During which season of the year does this poem probably take place?

A winter
B spring
C summer
D fall

HINT

The poem does not tell you when it takes place. But if you look at the poem, it is easy to see in line 2 that it took place "one cold day."

23 Poets sometimes give human qualities to animals or even to nonliving things. This is called *personification.* Tell how the poet uses personification in this poem.

___

___

___

___

___

24 What will the speaker do with the cat at the end of the poem? Tell about *two* pieces of evidence in the poem that support your answer.

HINT

Stories and poems on tests usually end happily for everyone. If you aren't sure, just read the last stanza again, especially the last two lines. When you write, be sure to answer both parts of the question. First, tell what will happen. Then give *two* pieces of evidence.

Family Heirlooms

by Russell Ross

Lev knocked on the door to his mother's room. "What is it, Lev?" she asked.

"I need to bring a family heirloom to school for a speech project," Lev answered. "Will you help me think of something?"

"I'm so sorry, sweetie," his mother said. "I have to put on my best business suit and go back to work for an important meeting. Mrs. Fine from next door is going to make dinner for you and Mila tonight, and she will stay with you if my meeting runs late. Can I help you tomorrow evening?"

Lev knew that tomorrow evening would be too late. His turn to present his speech about a family heirloom was tomorrow morning. He should have asked for help yesterday, but he had been too busy watching his favorite television shows. "Never mind," Lev said. "I'll ask Papa." But Lev soon learned that his father was out shopping for a new car. He probably wouldn't be home until late.

"Maybe Ivan will help me," Lev thought. But Lev's older brother was still at school. He was on the basketball team, and there was a game that night. He would not be home for hours. Lev's twin sister Mila was home, but could she help him? She had already made her presentation about a family heirloom in her own class. Her presentation was about the family's special tablecloth. It had come all the way from Russia. Their grandmother had brought it with her when she came to America years ago. Lev wanted his talk to be about something different, but he didn't know what.

Lev found Mila in the living room. She was on the couch looking at an album of photographs. Lev looked around the room. There was a painting that had also come all the way from Russia, but it was large and delicate, and very valuable. Lev would be afraid to bring it to school because it might get damaged. Lev realized there were many family heirlooms, such as his grandfather's violin and his grandmother's chest of drawers, but they were all too large or too valuable for him to be carrying around. Lev needed something that could fit easily into his book bag, the way the tablecloth had fit in Mila's book bag. His heirloom could be valuable, like the tablecloth, but not as valuable as the antique violin.

"Come look at these old pictures," Mila said to Lev. "Some of them show Mama and Papa when they were children. Some are even older. They show Grandma's house in Russia." Suddenly Lev was ecstatic because he knew just what his heirloom would be.

25 This story is mainly about a boy who wants someone to help him ______.

A shop for a new suit

B learn to play basketball

C make dinner for the family

D think of an idea for a school talk

HINT

All of these things are mentioned in the story, so you can't just skim through it. You must read it to find out which thing Lev was doing.

26 Lev's mother probably works in ______.

A a store

B a factory

C a restaurant

D an office building

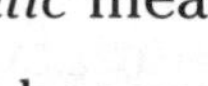

27 What does the word *ecstatic* mean in the sentence below?

Suddenly Lev was *ecstatic* because he knew just what his heirloom would be.

A angry

B excited

C surprised

D worried

HINT

How would *you* feel if something was bothering you, and then your problem was suddenly solved?

28 What was Lev's father doing that night?

- **A** staying late at work
- **B** shopping for a new car
- **C** visiting the next-door neighbor
- **D** watching his older son play basketball

29 Lev has to find something right away because ______.

- **A** he must give his speech the next morning
- **B** he wants to watch his favorite TV show
- **C** he doesn't want to wait until tomorrow evening
- **D** he wants to spend the next night writing his speech

30 The next day, Lev will probably go to school with a collection of old Russian ______.

- **A** violins
- **B** furniture
- **C** photographs
- **D** tablecloths

HINT

Which heirloom did Lev look at just before he decided?

31 Tell who spoke these words and what they mean in the story. Explain your answer completely.

"I have to put on my best business suit and go back to work for an important meeting."

____

____

____

____

____

____

32 The term *family heirloom* is used in the story. Explain what the author means by a family heirloom. Give at least *two* examples from the story to support your answer.

____

____

____

____

____

Soap Bubble Science

by Lee Chin

Introduction

This excellent activity is very popular. It provides great fun and science at the same time. You will need only the materials that are listed below. You will love performing and writing about this experiment.

Materials

Liquid dish detergent (some brands work better than others)
Cloth-covered wire pipe cleaners
Shallow metal or plastic pans
Plastic spoons
Water
Lots and lots of rags or paper towels
Pencils, pens, paper, and a ruler
A room without carpeting on the floor

Procedure

1 Pour an inch or two of water into a plastic pan.
2 Add a few drops of liquid dish detergent.
3 Stir the soap into the water.
4 Shape the pipe cleaner into a bubble wand.
5 Dip the wand into the water until a bubble covers the wand.
6 Move the handle of the wand through the air, or blow on it.
7 Keep notes about everything you do.

Your goals

Who can make the largest bubble?
Who can make the longest lasting bubble?
What can you learn from doing this activity?

Things to investigate

How much water and how much soap make the best mix?
What shape of bubble wand makes the best bubbles?
What technique for waving or blowing on the wand works best?

33 Which choice *best* tells what kind of selection this is?

- **A** instructions for an experiment
- **B** a chapter from a science book
- **C** directions for washing the dishes
- **D** a rainy-day arts and crafts project

> **HINT**
> This *could* be an activity in a science book, but there is a better answer.

34 The headings at the start of the main sections of this selection are made to stand out. This was done by printing these words using ______.

- **A** fancy type
- **B** underlining
- **C** capital letters
- **D** large, dark print

35 Which word could best take the place of the word *Procedure* as the heading of the numbered steps?

- **A** Rules
- **B** Follow-up
- **C** Directions
- **D** Suggestions

> **HINT**
> Look at those seven numbered steps. Which word *best* describes them?

36 What *probably* causes the soapy water to form into large bubbles?

- **A** stirring the soapy water
- **B** mixing soap into the water
- **C** moving air through the soapy water
- **D** touching the soapy water with a pipe cleaner

37 Which of these is *not* explained in the selection?

A What kind of soap should one use?

B What makes bubbles grow large and last long?

C What material should be used to make the bubble wand?

D What kind of container should be used for the soapy water?

HINT

The thing the author did not explain is something he wants students to investigate on their own.

38 Which numbered step tells how to actually form the bubbles?

A Step 2

B Step 4

C Step 6

D Step 7

39 This activity can be messy. Tell how it can make a mess. Also tell *two* things the author suggests doing to prevent or clean up a mess.

____

____

____

____

____

____

40 Look at the three questions under the last heading in the selection. How can a student investigate each of these things? Give at lease *two* examples to support your answer.

HINT

Your science knowledge will help you here. How do scientists learn new things? Be sure to give at least *two* examples.

____

____

____

____

____

____

____